ALCHEMISTS OF SUBURBIA

ALCHEMISTS OF SUBURBIA

A COURSE IN MIRACLES,
PSYCHOLOGY AND THE ART OF INTEGRATION

STEPHANIE PANAYI

Copyright © 2021 by Stephanie Panayi

All rights reserved. No part of this publication may be reproduced, stored or transmitted in any form or by any means, electronic, mechanical, photocopying, recording, scanning, or otherwise without written permission from the publisher. It is illegal to copy this book, post it to a website, or distribute it by any other means without permission.

Stephanie Panayi asserts the moral right to be identified as the author of this work.

Stephanie Panayi has no responsibility for the persistence or accuracy of URLs for external or third-party Internet Websites referred to in this publication and does not guarantee that any content on such Websites is, or will remain, accurate or appropriate.

All quotes are from A Course in Miracles, copyright ©1992, 1999, 2007 by the Foundation for Inner Peace, 448 Ignacio Blvd., #306, Novato, CA 94949, www.acim.org and info@acim.org, used with permission.

First edition

ISBN: 9798538442607

Everything that irritates us about others can lead us to an understanding of ourselves.

— Carl Gustav Jung

Contents

Preface	iii
The Inner Pilgrimage	1
The Thorn in Your Side	7
Pain and the Brain	10
Release the Hounds	13
The Present Memory	18
The Cookie Monster	23
The Jonah Complex and the Need to Belong	27
Dream Worlds	37
The Art of Listening	42
The Split—Part I: Freud, Jung and the Oceanic Feeling	48
The Split—Part II: Freud, Jung and the Oceanic Feeling	60
Through the Looking Glass: Forgiveness, Time and the Event Horizon	70
The Script Is Written: Synchronicity and the Mind-World Connection	77
Living Colour: Wholeness, Integration and Our One Self	82
Klein and A Course in Miracles: On Love, Loss and the Centrality of the Atonement Principle	92
Seeing the Problem as It Is—Part I: Karen Horney's Defensive Solutions	103
Seeing the Problem as It Is—Part II: Karen Horney's Defensive Solutions	112
Anxiety, Hostility and Unconditional Love	120
Play School: The World as Transitional Object	123
The Only True Reflection	131

In the Shadow of Gods—Part I: On Human Frailty and Self-Doubt	139
In the Shadow of Gods—Part II: On Human Frailty and Self-Doubt	144
Between the Sinner and the Saint—Part I: Hegel's Dialectic and Its Relationship to Healing	151
Between the Sinner and the Saint—Part II: Hegel's Dialectic and Its Relationship to Healing	157
Notes	167
About the Author	170
Also by Stephanie Panayi	171

Preface

Readers familiar with my earlier publications will know I like to look at philosophy, psychology and psychoanalytic theory alongside principles from *A Course in Miracles*. My aim is to make psychological concepts accessible, relatable and useful to the general reader and to students of the Course alike. For those unfamiliar with *A Course in Miracles*, I've provided a brief orientation later in this preface.

This volume of essays takes things up a notch or two on the psychoanalytic front and highlights a theme running through my first book *Above the Battleground: The Courageous Path to Emotional Autonomy and Inner Peace* — that embodying the wholeness of our personality runs alongside the progressive realisation of our spiritual Self. Forgiveness, then, can be thought of as a type of alchemy in which we own the discarded aspects of our innate personality by forgiving those we hold responsible for our self-alienation. Hence the title of this new volume, *Alchemists of Suburbia*.

My book *Reflections on* A Course in Miracles: *Volume Three*, contains two pieces on what I see as Freudian and Jungian aspects to the Course. I carry this theme into this present book, looking more closely at how Freud and Jung differ in their theories, and how their life experiences might have contributed to these differences.

It's all too easy to fall into a 'Freud versus Jung' dichotomy, whereby one figure is elevated and the other taken down regarding how their work contributes to (or detracts from) healing. A misunderstanding of Jung's analytical psychology might, for example, cause some people to neglect looking at aspects of their personal experience, such as past trauma, focusing on loftier, more esoteric concepts within Jungian psychology instead. This, however, wasn't Jung's intention. Jung emphasised the need to investigate past causes, and to address repressed memories as they emerged, and he was particularly concerned with issues related to our parents. Jung's major contribution was to *supplement* the exploration of past causes by a search for meaning and purpose. Why are the symptoms appearing *now*? What is the person trying to move *towards*, while feeling incapable or afraid of doing so?

Freudian theory, too, has been used in unhelpful ways, particularly his discovery that many problems relate to anxiety about a desire that breaks with social standards or rules. Some therapists concluded that the best way to deal with these conflicts was to strengthen the patient's defences against the desire, or to 'strengthen their ego' (the 'ego' in psychoanalysis being the mediator between our desires and their prohibitions). Many Ego Psychologists in the 1940s and 50s encouraged patients to conform to the mores of society, to gender expectations, sexual norms, and the prevailing ideas of what 'healthy' was: the *normal* family, the *normal* relationship, the *normal* role for your gender and age according to the majority. And so, therapy was designed to help people subdue whatever inner tendencies didn't fit with the norm, often encouraging them to identify with a mainstream structure such as an organised religion or a sporting team, supposedly strengthening their identity and ego in the process, but for many causing added stress and despair.

This approach contradicted Freud's own caution against set definitions of normality; he was in fact open to a wide variety of psychological solutions, believing that each person had a unique make-up and history, and their solutions could likewise be unique. Freud's emphasis wasn't on strengthening the ego, but on uncovering unconscious motivations and repressed memories. He assumed that the patient's ego would do whatever it had to do to acclimatise the patient to the change: his aim wasn't to impose a 'normal' identity onto a patient.

With this in mind, I hope the reader can find benefit in the contributions of both Freud and Jung towards an understanding of the human psyche and its motivations. Other notable theorists — Karen Horney, Melanie Klein, Donald Winnicott, and Jacques Lacan — also make an appearance. Their theories ground the Course's principles in everyday experience, illuminating their practical application. We take a look at Horney's defensive solutions to anxiety, Klein's exploration of the loss and depression associated with guilt, Winnicott's idea that transitional objects (à la children and their favourite blanket or soft toy) can help us bridge major thresholds of change, and Lacan's views on the role of language in shaping our sense of self. Lastly, the philosopher Georg Hegel brings us more closely to the concept of alchemy and the idea of reconciling opposites, leading to an expression of wholeness.

And of course, I take particular pleasure in discovering work by artists, writers and musicians that spark a line of enquiry. In this volume, you'll find homages to Kate Bush and Patti Smith: two artists who've had the courage to navigate their own path, and who've developed a genuine regard for their fellow travellers along the way.

Orientation: A Brief Tour of A Course in Miracles

A Course in Miracles is a psycho-spiritual book that aims to help us achieve inner peace. It's psychological in that it talks about psychological processes such as projection, repression, and integration, and focusses on the impact of our interpretations on our inner experience. It is also spiritual in its emphasis on a level of existence that lies beyond the world, beyond the body, outside time and space. The Course is a non-dualistic spiritual system because it says that only this spiritual level of existence is real, that the world and all of the chaos and destructiveness within it, is not. This is why the Course says that its central teaching can be summed up with the following:

> Nothing real can be threatened.
> Nothing unreal exists.
> Herein lies the peace of God.

The basic premise of the Course is that all of our dis-ease comes from identifying with our bodily experience within the world. A body can be threatened, hurt, abused, abandoned, and can in turn abuse, hurt and abandon others. It's a sad business. But, if despite all that goes on in our lives, we can connect with something within — a memory, a thought — that reflects the reality of the spiritual level of existence, we can then manage the trials and tribulations of our lives in a way that is most helpful to everyone, coming from love rather than fear. We can be 'in the world, but not of it' knowing that 'Nothing real can be threatened'. The aim isn't to deny our experience in the world, but to lessen our pain, to quieten our anxieties, and to be more open to our essential kinship with others.

From Unity to Opposition

Another major theme in *A Course in Miracles* is that of separation — that our experience in this world represents a belief that we have separated from God's Oneness. Feeling separate from our wholeness as part of a unified, spiritual Self, we feel incomplete (shameful) and sinful (guilty), imagining we have offended God.

If all of this talk of sin, guilt, and shame sounds a bit 'Biblical', it's intentional. The Course uses traditional Christian themes and terminology to help explain our psychological experience, but gives them a very different context and meaning. According to the Course, the Biblical story of Adam and Eve and their expulsion from Eden represents a *belief* about our relationship to God, not an actuality. The Course explores the origin of this belief through its own creation myth, and how to let it go through its unique definition of forgiveness.

Reinterpreting Symbols

The Course's language can be off-putting to some readers because it uses traditional Christian terms that have punitive and sacrificial connotations, general 'ye olde' language reminiscent of the Bible, and is full of masculine pronouns: He, brother, father, Sonship. There is, however, a method in this madness. The Bible-like form of the Course reflects its function as a correction for the Bible's exclusory and punitive teachings. Though it has been a source of guidance for many, the Bible has also contributed to a great deal of pain.

Minority groups, animals and the environment as a whole have long felt the brunt of the Bible's divisive passages. Humans are to have *dominion over the earth*; if you 'spare the rod' you 'spoil the child'; 'the head of woman is man': these are just a few Biblical statements that people have used to justify denigration and brutality. That the Bible is hardly a loving text in parts has proved troublesome for many of its followers. For example, it has been the subject of several books by the now retired American Episcopal Bishop John Shelby Spong. The title of his first book speaks volumes about his difficulties with the Bible: *Here I Stand: My Struggle for a Christianity of Integrity, Love and Equality*.

The Course's use of masculine pronouns, historically a practice related to a general disregard of women, is a way of bringing to light the need for such attitudes to be corrected and the wounds around them healed. We read the exclusive words, we notice they bite, our issues are brought to the surface. Even the word 'God' and referring to Him as a 'He' can bring up thoughts of a punitive father, a distant overlord. (For more on the gendered issue of God, I refer the interested reader to the last chapter in my book *Reflections on* A Course in Miracles: *Volume Three*).

That being said, though the Course uses the exclusive, gendered form but gives it an inclusive content (for example, 'Brother' in the Course, also means 'sister', 'non-binary individual', 'every person'), that doesn't mean we should repeat the stylistic errors of the past, and so I have tried to be as inclusive as I can with my language. However, for the sake of consistency and clarity, I refer to 'He' when referencing symbols from the Course that use that pronoun. With all of this in mind, the following are some more 'loaded' words with their distinct Course definitions.

Atonement: The Course uses the term 'Atonement Principle' for the idea that we have never separated from God, that we have nothing to 'atone' for in terms of having offended Him in some way. In contrast, 'atonement' in the Bible relates to having to make up for a transgression against God in order to be saved from eternal suffering.

Christ: refers to our whole, spiritual Self, our true identity as part of Oneness. This is in contrast to the Biblical use in which Christ refers only to Jesus.

Ego: the belief in the false self — the self, separated from God.

Forgiveness: occurs when we realise our wholeness can't be affected by anyone or anything. We no longer blame someone else for our lack of peace in the here and now. The Course's path to healing and inner peace.

God: the Creator of an abstract unity of love of which our spiritual Self is a part.

Guilt: all the negative feelings and beliefs we have about ourselves, including shame.

Scarcity Principle: Believing we have separated from Oneness, we feel empty and incomplete. We try and find fulfillment in special people, projects, careers, accumulating money, anything that is outside of ourselves.

Holy Spirit: the memory of our spiritual Self and wholeness. A bridge between our identity as a (guilty, shameful) ego self in time, and our reality as a completely whole and innocent spiritual Self in eternity.

Miracle: when we accept that the cause of our dis-ease is our having identified with the ego, and then listen to the Holy Spirit's message of wholeness instead.

Sin: the belief we turned our back on God's Oneness and love, separating from Him so we could live a life of our own. We then experience guilt and a fear of God's retribution.

Special Relationships: Relationships through which we try to make up for our feelings of incompleteness are called 'special love' relationships. 'Special hate' relationships are those in which we try to get rid of our guilt by projecting it onto others.

I hope this provides sufficient orientation for those unfamiliar with *A Course in Miracles*. If you feel the need for a more in-depth discussion of the Course's metaphysical basis before diving in, I recommend beginning at the chapter titled 'Dream Worlds', where you'll get an overview of the creation myth at the heart of the Course's teachings.

Regarding the referencing system, the Course has a text (T), workbook of lessons (W), manual (M), clarification of terms (C), psychotherapy pamphlet (P) and prayer pamphlet (S). The following example shows how the references are to be read:

'What could correct for separation but its opposite?' T-28.VII.2:6.

T = Text, 28 = Chapter 28, VII = Section VII, 2 = Paragraph 2, 6 = Line 6

The Inner Pilgrimage

The word pilgrim is derived from the Latin, *peregrinus*, meaning foreigner or stranger. Pilgrims are people who've travelled from afar to reach a destination promising some kind of answer. Traditionally, these destinations have a religious significance, and the long, arduous journey towards them becomes a metaphor for an inner process; a preparation for the hoped-for change to come. Perhaps we want to feel free of a burden of guilt that we've carried for many years, the strenuous journey a means of expiating our sin or a sign of our dedication. Upon arrival at the place of spiritual significance, we might receive a blessing and can return to our lives born anew.

Ancient pilgrimage trails are now popular tourist destinations, and not everyone embarks on them for spiritual reasons. Some might wish to enjoy new landscapes and cultures whilst being active. Others still walk with a greater purpose in mind: to deal with grief over the loss of a loved one, or the end of a relationship. Whatever the reason, people often undertake a pilgrimage when a real shift is desired, needed, or about to occur, and that shift will often involve reviewing our self-concept.

The nature of every relationship we have within the world — with colleagues, family members, partners, projects and careers — is influenced by beliefs about who we are. In the first half of life, it is natural and unavoidable for these beliefs to be tightly bound to what we *do* in the world; to our roles at home, work and within society as a whole. Around mid-life, these identifications get challenged. Children leave home, businesses close down, our physical capacities change, and a host of unforeseen circumstances can turn our lives upside down. Who are we then, when we wake up in the morning without a role to frame the day and give us direction?

The angst involved in asking this question is well known to professional athletes who've lived life according to a strict routine and narrowly defined purpose from an early age. For the Olympic swimmer in training, following the long, black line in the pool literally gives them a direction that they don't have to reconsider for many years. Society tells them that the goal of Olympic glory is worthwhile, prized even. Sponsorship deals, celebrity status and an adoring fanbase give no reason to question the value of their dedication. And so it is with many things: the world tells us particular roles can make us happy, or at least keep us going. And for a time, they seem to do just that.

We experience a reckoning in the second half of life when, for whatever reason, we can't proceed along the path we've been accustomed to. Watching a television programme about a group's pilgrimage to Rome, I was struck by the experience of an ex-Olympic athlete who expressed his difficulty in dealing with this stage. 'I don't know what I am', he said, then began to tear-up. This reminded me of the following passage from *A Course in Miracles*, in the section 'Self-Concept versus Self':

> There will come a time when images have all gone by, and you will see you know not what you are... There is no statement that the world is more afraid to hear than this: I do not know the thing I am, and therefore do not know what I am doing, where I am, or how to look upon the world or on myself.[1]

Another example of this existential crisis involves a woman who was forever trying to manage the behaviour of her ten-year-old son, Jordan, who had Attention Deficit Hyperactivity Disorder (ADHD). After several trips to alternative and traditional medical experts, and many failed behavioural schemes and diets to alter Jordan's behaviour, the mother was at her wits end. Her days were a constant battle to get Jordan to do just about anything, including going to school. In desperation she sought the advice of another specialist, and after following the suggested treatment the results were dramatic. Jordan was able to concentrate at school and better tolerate his emotions. His grades improved along with his behaviour and home became a more peaceful place.

The most interesting part of this story lies in the mother's response to the new normal: she felt lost. Her days had been occupied with trying to handle Jordan, and now that his behaviour was no longer a problem, she felt she'd lost a sense of purpose. What was she *for* if she wasn't to be a full-time manager of her son? Despite how painful it had been to deal with Jordan's problematic behaviour, the feeling of being adrift seemed worse. The Course tells us that, though these moments of self-doubt — of not knowing what we are — are very painful, they are our way out of misery because they open our mind to an awareness of our spiritual Self:

> Yet in this learning is salvation born. And What you are will tell you of Itself.[2]

> It is to this unsealed and open mind that truth returns, unhindered and unbound. Where concepts of the self have been laid by is truth revealed exactly as it is. When every concept has been raised to doubt and question, and been recognized as made on no assumptions that would stand the light, then is the truth left free to enter in its sanctuary, clean and free of guilt.[3]

If this time of questioning leads us to such a positive conclusion, we might ask why it feels so awful. Why do we struggle so much with letting go of our roles? Why do we tear-up at the thought of not knowing what we are?

Contrary to what we believe, our real fear isn't of not having a purpose per se, but of what a more open, unclouded mind — free of fixed self-concepts and their attendant noise — would feel like. We are, the Course tells us, ultimately afraid of redemption, which sounds counter-intuitive. Why on earth would we fear having a peaceful inner experience, 'clean and free of guilt'? Simply stated, it's because there's no 'I' in peace, no special self, no distinction between ourselves and God's Love:

> We have said that no one will countenance fear if he recognises it. Yet in your disordered state of mind you are not afraid of fear. You do not like it, but it is not your desire to attack that really frightens you… you are more afraid of what it covers… Your real terror is of redemption.[4]

> Under the ego's dark foundation is the memory of God, and it is of this that you are really afraid. For this memory would instantly restore you to your proper place, and it is this place that you have sought to leave. Your fear of attack is nothing compared to your fear of love.[5]

We fear love because we want to be the ego self we made, instead of the Self that God created: we don't want to avail ourselves of a love that is not of our making.

The Course assures us that we won't lose anything of value as we practice letting go of our ego. On the contrary, we'll become more peaceful, happy and certain. It takes us a while, however, to develop trust that this will be the case. Until then, the temptation is to try and establish another self-concept to replace the one that has 'gone into retirement'. We become just as obsessed and fixated on another goal, another charity, another project or cause to give us direction.

To move forward, we need to shift our emphasis from what we do to Who we do it with. Will we do it with the ego or the Holy Spirit as our guide? Will we do it with a sense of competition, indulging judgements of 'good' and 'bad', or will we let concepts of ourselves and of others take a back seat, leaving the way open to be a vehicle for Love's extension? In any given moment, the only meaningful thing we can do is to remember our shared need to know of the innocence and safety of our spiritual Self. This purpose might lead us to be attracted to certain occupations and relationships, but what we do is now secondary to this higher aim.

Whenever we find ourselves obsessed with a task, forgetting Who is always with us, we can be sure we have stepped into a self-concept — a bodily identification — that will have us focused on the world of form, taking our 'doing' seriously, forgetting that the real source of healing comes from an acceptance of the Atonement Principle — our holiness — within our minds. It's only when we remember that we need do nothing for our salvation and the salvation of others that we can be of real help. In turn, the peace in our minds becomes a reminder to others of the same holiness within their own. To carry a sense of rest in all our busy doings is the way to move forward from self-concepts altogether:

> To do nothing is to rest, and make a place within you where the activity of the body ceases to demand attention. Into this place the Holy Spirit comes, and there abides. He will remain when you forget, and the body's activities return to occupy your conscious mind.
>
> Yet there will always be this place of rest to which you can return. And you will be more aware of this quiet centre of the storm than all its raging activity. This quiet centre, in which you do nothing, will remain with you, giving you rest in the midst of every busy doing on which you are sent.[6]

This sense of rest establishes our innocence, freeing us of every self-concept the ego would deploy as a defence against guilt and shame. The second half of life is a time of liberation begun with a pilgrimage, a long process of letting go and tolerating uncertainty, to be rewarded with a new life in awareness of a mighty Companion Who has never left our side. We need only stay strong, keep to the 'straight and narrow' path, and not look back, for it's in our dedication that our success is assured.

The Thorn in Your Side

Shakespeare and the Bible: many terms we use in everyday speech originate from these two sources. 'Faint hearted', for example, is a phrase from *Henry VI*, as is 'Dead as a doornail'. 'Thorn in my side' has that pithy, punchy Shakespearean quality about it, but it wasn't coined by the great bard. It comes from that extremely well travelled apostle, Saint Paul.

The exact words Paul used were 'thorn in my flesh', but they've been adapted over time. Today we use the phrase to describe something that is a persistent trouble, a source of pain and distress. You might recall the Eurythmics hit from the eighties about an unfaithful ex. No one, however, really knows what Saint Paul was referring to in his letter to the Corinthians, but it has been suggested the thorn was some form of impiety; perhaps one of the seven deadly sins: lust, greed, gluttony and the rest. Or perhaps Paul's thorn was a general disagreeableness or lack of charity towards others. Whatever it was, Paul prayed for the thorn to be removed, but it remained.

And so, Paul reconciled himself with the thorn by giving it a higher purpose — what we do know about is Paul's positive spin on having this source of perpetual annoyance: 'And lest I should be exalted above measure through the abundance of the revelations, there was given to me a thorn in the flesh ...' Saint Paul decided that the metaphorical thorn kept him grounded, bringing him down to earth in case he developed an inflated sense of 'spiritual specialness' from the insights he was receiving.

But he goes on: 'For this thing I besought the Lord thrice, that it might depart from me. And he said unto me, "My grace is sufficient for thee: for my strength is made perfect in weakness". Most gladly therefore will I rather glory in my infirmities, that the power of Christ may rest upon me'. Paul's thorn — his weakness — would remind him that any strength he ever showed was not *of* him but came *through* him. The saint reasoned his weakness into a strength because through it he would remember where true strength lies.

Like Paul and his impiety, we can find ourselves lacking any one of the qualities outlined in the manual of *A Course in Miracles* which we're said to embody more as we progress with our practice of forgiveness. Qualities such as patience, gentleness, kindness and tolerance are ideals that can seem unreachable in particular circumstances, with particular people, or just simply on a bad day. Try as we might, we can't shake our impatience, our frustration, our ingratitude. Rather than feeling like a failure, however, or lamenting the persistence of our dis-ease, we can use it as a reminder that we're not alone.

Our limitations remind us what the problem is (that we think we're separate, a power unto ourselves) and what the solution is (remembering God). It is through this process that we can *rest* in God, becoming more patient, tolerant and kind to ourselves.

> Do not despair, then, because of limitations. It is your function to escape from them, but not to be without them.[7]

It is our function to remember what the real problem and solution is. A limitation — a thorn — provides us with this opportunity. If we were without limitations altogether — if we were totally ego-free — we wouldn't be able to be here:

> Sometimes a teacher of God may have a brief experience of direct union with God. In this world, it is almost impossible that this endure.[8]

Instead of feeling guilty for our limitations, we can use them as a reminder of the happy truth: a greater strength travels with us. We might still feel the thorn, but it won't preoccupy us because it no longer serves the ego's purpose of distracting us from love.

Pain and the Brain

Pain. It can stop us in our tracks, preoccupy our thoughts and root our attention to our body. Physiologically speaking, we feel pain only when our brain perceives a threat. You can stub your toe, for example, but unless your brain receives enough information (namely from chemical messengers released at the site of impact) conveying that your toe needs repair, you won't experience pain.

The brain's central role in pain perception is particularly intriguing when it comes to chronic pain with no apparent cause, there doesn't seem to be any reason for the pain (there's no tissue damage, for example) but the brain has nonetheless decided that a certain part of the body is in trouble, and so issues the 'pain' order.

Complex Regional Pain Syndrome (CRPS) is a condition that can occur in such a scenario. Not only does a person develop chronic pain in an area, but the brain instigates an inflammatory response there, causing swelling and further restriction of movement. Sometimes, CRPS develops after a minor injury, such as a sprained ankle. The brain seems to go into 'over-protective parent' mode, issuing a response that is excessive and relentless.

No one knows the exact cause of CRPS or of many other chronic pain conditions, but the latest neuroscience research suggests that our thoughts play a significant role. Catastrophic thinking, or catastrophising, ('I can't stand it!', 'It's going to get worse!', or 'I'll never be rid of it') amplifies chronic pain. This makes sense when you understand that the brain's pain response is proportional to the degree of threat it perceives, and that our thoughts contribute to such perception. If there's one thing I remember from my

First Aid training, it's to be as calm and reassuring as you can when helping someone out, as this can lessen their distress and experience of pain.

From the point of view of *A Course in Miracles*, catastrophic thinking is related to guilt over separating from God, and a fear of retribution: If we believe we are a guilty, ego self, then we'll also believe that things are going to get worse for us. When we think like this, our pain, our suffering, increases: as masochistic as it might sound, suffering holds some attraction in that it mitigates our fear of something worse happening to us further down the track. *If God sees how much I'm suffering now, surely He won't punish me for the 'sin' of separation.*

So, how might we approach chronic pain from a Course point of view? The Course tells us that everything we experience reflects a decision: to identify with either our ego or with our spiritual Self; to believe in separation or unity, in guilt or innocence. Ultimately, this decision leads to feeling threatened or safe. Catastrophic thinking is then a reflection of choosing to identify with the ego, and hence pain. This is, naturally, an intrusion on our peace.

Importantly, however, it's not the case that we should be pain free if we have chosen to listen to the Holy Spirit and remember our Self. Like any other feeling, pain can be used to root us in the world, or to remember our true Identity as spirit. Pain, per se, isn't the problem. Just as we can feel hungry, hot, tired or cold, we can feel pain, which is really another type of discomfort. And just as feeling hungry isn't an indication that you're in your wrong mind, neither is experiencing pain or taking medication for it. It's what we do with our discomfort — how we interpret it — that can either let it move into the background of our experience or take centre stage. In other words, what will we use the pain *for*? We are always setting a goal as to what we want to emphasise about ourselves and the world, and this will determine our inner experience:

> In any situation in which you are uncertain, the first thing to consider, very simply, is 'What do I want to come of this? What is it for?' The clarification of the goal belongs at the beginning, for it is

this which will determine the outcome. In the ego's procedure this is reversed. The situation becomes the determiner of the outcome...[9]

The ego's goal is to keep us from our mind (where our power lies) by trying to convince us that the body and the world are the causes of our distress (and our pleasure). This serves the ego's purpose nicely: it makes the world very real in our experience, along with the past, the body, and our sense of victimisation (whether at the hands of another person, a bug or our own 'foolish' actions). Our thoughts have no role to play in pain if we believe the situation determines the outcome. Like the brain, the ego would have us believe that the intensity of our pain is proportional to the amount of damage done to us. But the brain gets it wrong, and so does the ego. To the ego, pain says the world is real and God's unity is dead. That's a scary, catastrophic, thought.

If, however, we make our goal to remember who we are, we can ask the Holy Spirit to help us look at our pain without fear. And as we choose to release everyone from any guilt surrounding this pain, we allow the pain to recede into the background. Maybe we associate our pain with having been overworked, neglected, abused or unsupported. Or maybe it's the 'straw that broke the camel's back' in terms of all we have endured in our life generally. The Holy Spirit looks on our pain and says, 'not one note in Heaven's song was missed'.[2] We are not damaged, in danger or a prisoner to what we have done or has been done to us.

Our goal, then, isn't so much to be pain-free, but to let go of guilt and grievances — then our pain won't be exacerbated. And as it loses its ability to distract us from the Holy Spirit's answer (a remembrance of our holiness and eternal safety), our pain may indeed go altogether at times, but it won't be a big deal either way: forgiveness and peace will be the outcome, and we'll be able to do (or stop doing) whatever it is that would constitute moving forward.

Release the Hounds

I'm a big fan of Kate Bush, the English singer/songwriter who emerged on the music scene in the late Seventies. I don't own the whole catalogue of her music; just a few tracks which I really love. One of those tracks is 'Hounds of Love'. The recording starts with a man sounding desperate and alarmed: 'It's in the trees! It's coming!' This sets the scene: the hounds of love are something to be feared.

The song is about being afraid to fall in love because of the pain and confusion that accompanies relationships. Said Bush in an interview (*Conversation Disc Series*, 1985):

> The ideas for 'Hounds of Love', the title track, are very much to do with love itself and people being afraid of it, the idea of wanting to run away from love, not to let love catch them, and trap them, in case the hounds might want to tear them to pieces and it's very much using the imagery of love as something coming to get you and you've got to run away from it or you won't survive.

The Hungry Dogs of Fear

One of the most dramatic passages in *A Course in Miracles* also uses the imagery of hounds frantically seeking out their prey. It occurs in the section 'The Obstacles to Peace' in which we're told that the first obstacle to peace is our desire to get rid of it. While we might think we want peace, we don't want to lose the specialness of our separate, ego self. We want to stay away from God, and that means — despite our protestations to the contrary — that we *don't* want the peace of God.

This resistance to peace is expressed through a grievance; the '...little remnant of attack you cherish still against your brother'. We might have been working with the Course for many years, having let go of a lot of 'stuff', yet there are likely to be a few choice grievances that still serve as effective defences against peace. We cherish these 'little barriers of sand', these 'walls of dust', because they seem to be limited in scope, well circumscribed and isolated — to oppose God's Will by 'a little' limits our awareness of the Whole as much as opposing it by 'a lot'. Saint John of the Cross had a great analogy for this: just as a bird tied to a branch by five pieces of string still can't fly away if four pieces are cut, so too are we bound to our ego-identification if we cherish one 'scrap of evil', one 'microscopic remnant of the belief in sin'.

When we choose against God's Will and for the ego instead, the fear we experience has us looking for a scapegoat onto whom we can project our guilt. We experience a great emotional need to blame something else for our lack of peace: we need to perceive a perpetrator so we can feel morally superior and abate our fear. The Course talks about fear's messengers — the 'hungry dogs of fear' — being sent out in a 'savage search for sin':

> The messengers of fear are harshly ordered to seek out guilt, and cherish every scrap of evil and of sin that they can find...
> No little shred of guilt escapes their hungry eyes. And in their savage search for sin they pounce on any living thing they see, and carry it screaming to their master, to be devoured.[10]

In essence, fear's messengers return with 'word of bones and skin and flesh', which means that we only see evidence confirming that someone is a body; limited to the insecurities, aggression and complexities of human nature. If you are nothing more than the domineering, insensitive, jealous, unreasonable, self-centred (fill in the blank) person I think you are, then I too am only a body.

To equate ourselves with the body leads to depression because it denies the wholeness of our spiritual Self and the reality of God's unchanging Oneness. The body's senses speak of differentiation, opposites and mortality. Rooting our identity to the body therefore makes the thought of death and destruction real, and the reality of God's love a thing of fantasy. Feeling depressed, however, we don't recognise the cause and attribute it instead to the grievance at hand, thus perpetuating a vicious cycle: *I was angry because of what you did, and now I'm depressed because of it too!*

The little remnant we hold against someone can thereby develop a life of its own, growing as our pain and depression grows, along with our chants of 'If only!' We believe the grass would be greener if some aspect of our outer existence changed. From the perspective of the Holy Spirit, which sees the illusory nature of anything less than the wholeness of our spiritual Self, there is only ever one answer for a lack of peace *right now*:

> There is no order of difficulty in Miracles, for they are all the same. Each is a gentle winning over from the appeal of guilt to the appeal of love…[11]

The Messengers of Love

While guilt and fear motivate us to send out messengers in search of sin, the Holy Spirit would give us love's messengers to send instead. These would help us to see beyond the body — beyond differences and the form of someone's behaviour — to the call for help behind an attack. Often, this is a call that echoes our own, having believed we separated from love. In this recognition of our mutual interest, our focus moves beyond what has been said and done to our shared spiritual need.

Love's messengers help us to become more balanced in our perceptions. The ego's blinkered sight seeks for sin and ignores any evidence to the contrary, leading to painful misunderstandings. I suspect we've all had the experience of saying something without malice or an intention to demean, but been met with a totally unexpected response of fury or indignation as if what we'd said was an attack. If someone's identified with their ego, they'll be feeling defensive, and fear's messengers will find anything to blame for their dis-ease. Love's messengers focus on something entirely different:

> They will be as careful to let no little act of charity, no tiny expression of forgiveness, no little breath of love escape their notice.[12]

If we don't fixate on the ego in others, if we're willing to see something as a mistake rather than condemn it as sin, we'll also release Love's messengers and our perceptions will shift. Love's messengers, however, can be experienced as fearful — as baying hounds — because they would herald the end of our special self and the special 'love-hate' nature of our relationships. As the Course states:

> Future loss is not your fear. But present joining is your dread.[13]

We might fear the future pain inherent in all relationships, but our real fear is of the potential for joining:

For if they joined each one would lose its own identity, and by their separation are their selves maintained.[14]

We're also told that only minds can join, so the issue isn't whether we end up in a physical, intimate, relationship with someone, but whether we're willing to accept our unity with others by recognising our foundational sameness.

So, while we think we fear the pain of relationships — of being torn apart by the 'hounds of love' — our real fear is of letting go of guilt and embracing the innocence of our Self:

> You are not really afraid of crucifixion. Your real terror is of redemption.[15]

As Kate Bush laments throughout 'Hounds of Love', 'I don't know what's good for me, I don't know what's good for me'. We can think that the best thing for our happiness is to stay away from relationships because of the pain they elicit, but relationships — in particular, the way we perceive and respond to others — also offer us endless opportunities to undo projection and become aware of our guilt, enabling us to undo it through forgiveness. Ultimately, whether we experience them as a hindrance or as an asset in our search for peace depends on which messengers we choose to send forth, and this in turn depends on what our goal is: to reinforce perceptions of guilt and victimisation, or to awaken to the holiness we share.

The Present Memory

Several years ago, I had an experience in my Rolfing® (bodywork) clinic that has stayed with me as a poignant example of the Course's definition of 'Miracle'. Part of my clinical practice involved seeing children with Global Developmental Delay (GDD), meaning they experienced significant delays across multiple developmental milestones such as walking, talking and eating solid foods. Many children with GDD also display autistic traits, such as sensitivity to sensory stimulation and a reluctance to engage with others.

I loved working with these children, although it was challenging at times. No doubt a large part of my enjoyment came from the unique dynamic created by the participation of a parent: since most of the children with GDD were unable to follow instructions, I needed a parent to help me position them and, more importantly, to elicit their co-operation. This could be tricky. If a child was in an 'I'm not having it!' mood, an errant kick, punch or even a bite might hit its target — me.

One particular morning, Oliver was in such a mood. Before the session began his father, Gary, told me that two days previous, Oliver had lashed out at a radiographer who was trying to position him for a scan. The radiographer retaliated by becoming rough, at which point Gary said to him, 'Mate, if you carry on like that with Oliver, you're going to have trouble with *me!*' I could easily see how this could happen: when Oliver wouldn't co-operate, it seemed to have a personal sting. The scenario had clearly disturbed Gary as it was still prominent in his mind.

We began the treatment and sure enough, Oliver started to protest. I was gently working on his ankle with him semi-reclined on the treatment table, when I noticed his eyes fixate on my arm. In that split moment I knew Oliver was going to aggressively grab at my hand to pull it away from his leg, and so did Gary: 'Ollie', he cautioned sternly.

Around that same moment, without any conscious intention, I tuned into the music playing softly in the background. I don't recall the exact track but it was a very familiar classical piece. And as Oliver reached towards my hand, I let go of his leg and met him part-way, taking his hand gently and effortlessly moving it in time with the music as I looked at him and sang along, 'Da-dum, da-dum, da-dum'. It was 'a moment', one in which Oliver had let me join with him through the music. Gary shot a stunned look at me, and then at Oliver. Nothing was said, but I resumed the treatment with no further resistance.

What struck me most about this encounter was the absolute lack of effort or conscious intention on my part to do what I did: it just happened. I also didn't hesitate to do it, not feeling an ounce of doubt along the way. This is an example of what being in the present moment — free of past associations ('Here we go again: Oliver's being difficult') and of wondering whether to do 'this' or 'that' — truly means. It also exemplifies what a Miracle is: it's the moment we choose to identify with the Holy Spirit's thought system of unity and love instead of the ego's thought system of guilt and separate/competing interests.

The moment I knew Oliver was feeling confrontational and intended to grab my hand, I could have seen myself at odds with him; a victim, put-out, perhaps even offended. Though I wasn't aware of any conscious request for the Holy Spirit's help, I must have turned within to receive it, and the answer came in the form of my joining with the music and then using it to join with Oliver. I was able to do this because I was willing to let go of my special, ego-self, and its 'you versus me' thought system. In the split second between noticing Oliver reach for my hand and me taking his, I had lost my fear of joining:

> Everyone has experienced what he would call a sense of being

transported beyond himself... It is a sense of actual escape from limitations... it is a sudden unawareness of the body, and a joining of yourself and something else in which your mind enlarges to encompass it. It becomes part of you, as you unite with it. And both become whole, as neither is perceived as separate. What really happens is that you have given up the illusion of a limited awareness, and lost your fear of union.[16]

From Time to Timelessness

Forgiveness, as the Course tells us, offers everything we want, and the Course's 'holy instant' is a moment in which we step out of the chain of time by practicing forgiveness. The holy instant is an experience of 'the now' that doesn't know of past or future, but refers to our timeless reality, and we approach it with a focus on shared interests instead of competing interests; brothers and sisters instead of victims and victimisers — it's what I experienced in that moment with Oliver.

The present moment, as commonly understood, is something different to the holy instant. The present moment relates to this moment, *here within the chain of time*. Many Eastern philosophical traditions have practices designed to keep our attention in the present moment; the only time that actually *is*. In Buddhist mindfulness practice, for example, the aim is not to dwell on the past, the future or any thought, but to concentrate on some aspect of what is happening in the present, such as your breath, your steps as you walk, or the food you are eating. This can be a helpful exercise for many people. It can be calming, and helps to train the mind to let go of the very human habit of becoming lost in reactivity, our minds jumping around like an agitated monkey.

Mindfulness training is an exercise for 'toning' the mind. There is, however, still a degree of self-consciousness; a sense of an 'I' who his doing the exercise. When we are in the Course's holy instant, there is no effort at all: we are connected with our timeless Self and experience a certainty based on Love's free extension. You could say that while bringing our mind to the present moment is an activity related to the horizontal dimension of time, an experience of the holy instant relates to the vertical dimension in which we transcend time completely:

> In the longitudinal or horizontal plane the recognition of the equality of the members of the Sonship appears to involve almost endless time. However, the Miracle entails a sudden shift from horizontal to vertical perception. This introduces an interval from which the giver and receiver both emerge farther along in time than they would otherwise have been… It [the Miracle] does so by the underlying recognition of perfect equality of giver and receiver on which the Miracle rests.[17]

In terms of the Course's curriculum, the value of bringing our mind back to the present moment (which returns our attention to our mind) is that we can then avail ourselves of the 'present memory' in which we remember our oneness with God and with each other. When our mind wanders into the world, into the past or future, into getting something or avoiding it, into grievances and judgements, we can gently bring it back into the present so as to remember Who walks with us, and that we're all in the same boat — we all share the same pain of the ego thought system and the same need to remember the innocence of our spiritual Self.

Indeed, two major themes that run through the Course's *Manual for Teachers* are the importance of seeing shared interests instead of separate interests and of turning inward for help from our Inner Teacher. If we keep these two themes in mind throughout our day, we will be well on the path to experiencing the holy instant as our only instant; a space in which we unselfconsciously live in the present. Without identifying with a sinful past, or a fearful future, we are able to truly rest within the certainty of our

Holiness:

> Only uncertainty can be defensive. And all uncertainty is doubt about yourself.[18]

What then remains is an uninhibited flow of love's extension that is not of this world. We can't accomplish this alone, but we don't have to:

> He joins with you to make the holy instant far greater than you can understand. It is your realisation that you need do so little that enables Him to give so much.[19]

The Cookie Monster

Yesterday I went to the dentist for a routine check-up. The prospect of reclining in the dentist's chair is never a pleasant one for me, and so I appreciate the small talk I have with the receptionist while I wait. Yesterday's topic: 'The Terrible Twos'. The receptionist told me her daughter had just turned two and was displaying the classic defiance associated with that age. 'It actually started when she was eighteen months old', she confided. 'She throws herself on the ground, screams and kicks about. I'm just glad she hasn't done it in public yet. What would I do if she did it in the supermarket?! We don't give her lots of attention when she has a tantrum, because if you do…'

'It gets worse', I said, thinking I was completing her sentence in agreement.

'It gets worse?!' The receptionist looked at me, horrified. I knew she had misunderstood me to mean that things generally get worse as time goes by.

'No, I mean, it gets worse if you give them lots of attention in that moment because then they'll do it more often'. As the sage advice goes, when a toddler throws themselves onto the floor, screaming and kicking, the best thing to do is to calmly walk around them.

Likewise, though it's important to look at our ego — to notice when we are comparing, judging and generally indulging in specialness — it is also important not to match the intensity of our ego reactions with an equal amount of attention in order to overcome them. Lesson 123 in the Course's Workbook provides an example of how we can 'walk around' our ego tantrums:

> Today let us be thankful. We have come to gentler pathways and to smoother roads. There is no thought of turning back, and no implacable resistance to the truth. A bit of wavering remains, some small objections and a little hesitance, but you can well be grateful for your gains, which are far greater than you realise.
>
> A day devoted now to gratitude will add the benefit of some insight into the real extent of all the gains which you have made; the gifts you have received.[20]

In other words, we can apply some perspective to what we are experiencing. Rather than an intense state of disquiet being a sign of a big deal — something in need of some serious work — we can see it as 'a bit of wavering', 'a little resistance to the truth'. We can develop a nonchalant attitude as we replace the intensity of our guilt with gratitude for how far we've come — if we're willing to be wrong about our insistence that the source of our distress is outside of us, then we have indeed come a long way. The problem is that the more we let go of guilt the more our ego attacks stand out, and so we can mistakenly think we've gone backwards. As the Course points out, it's not wise to put ourselves in charge of judging our progress, because we don't know advance from retreat.

We all have issues that need an airing at times, and working through several aspects of a grievance is often necessary to bring hidden beliefs about ourselves to light. Sometimes, a sensitive working-through with a therapist can be extremely helpful in this regard. The ego's tantrum aspect becomes relevant when a grievance or belief persists despite having been given considerable attention in order to move beyond it ('Haven't I dealt with this already?!' we're prone to ask ourselves). This is because the ego likes to keep every speck of hurt handy to use whenever we turn our back on the Holy Spirit. In such circumstances we identify with our ego instead; we displace the true source of our pain onto these specks to distract us from the source within our minds, and to defend us from guilt:

The doubtful service of such displacement is to hide the real source of guilt... You are therefore willing to look upon all kinds of 'sources,' provided they are not the deeper source to which they bear no real relationship at all.[21]

We can think of these specks of hurt as cookies, and we feed on them to assuage our guilt and maintain our ego identity. We have a box of favourites, of 'allsorts', a selection of the tastiest grievances, which are most easily digested and never fail to satisfy. The Holy Spirit also has a selection of memories, but they would never make us sick from over indulgence. They are 'only the loving thoughts we have given and those that were given us':

All the rest must be forgotten. Forgiveness is a selective remembering, based not on your selection.[22]

When I was sixteen, I worked as a nanny in the school holidays. Three days a week I looked after Rowan, a two-year-old with a voracious appetite for cookies. I was under strict instructions from Rowan's mother: Rowan was only allowed to have two cookies a day, no matter how much he carried on. And so, every time Rowan threw himself on the floor in protest against the 'third cookie' embargo, I calmly walked around him and did whatever else I had to do. It was amazing how the tears and screams could stop as suddenly as they had started. Some days took more perseverance than others, but generally the strategy worked.

One day when the holidays had ended and I arrived at Rowan's to collect my pay, his father answered the door and let me in. As we walked past the kitchen which opened into the dining room, I saw Rowan sitting on the kitchen floor, his back leaning against a cupboard, his legs stretched out in front of him with a large jar of cookies nestled between them. He was in the process of putting a cookie into his mouth as I passed by.

'Hi Rowan', I said, a little surprised by the scene before me.

'Hi Step', Rowan replied, not yet having mastered the pronunciation of 'eph'.

I chatted for a while with Rowan's father in the dining room then headed past the kitchen again as I was leaving. 'See you, Rowan', I said as I passed. Rowan was still hoeing into the cookies but he seemed bored.

'See ya, Step'. That made me smile: 'See ya' — the use of that adult phrase. And just like an adult, he had that 'non-plussed' look you get from not feeling very engaged with anything: apart from the repetitive movement of hand into cookie jar, cookie into mouth, Rowan seemed removed. And so it is with all of us when we over indulge in our Grievance Allsorts. We become bored, we don't feel good, life loses its lustre.

The silver lining to over-indulging is that you get a clear picture of where a particular behaviour or thought leads. We can then use this experience to motivate us to choose differently next time; to walk around our ego in acknowledgement that we don't want to go where it's taking us. We can say, 'I don't want this', and ask for help from the Holy Spirit to choose peace instead of our separate, ego identity. We can step away from the cookie jar in recognition that, to paraphrase the Course, forgiveness gives us everything we want.

The Jonah Complex and the Need to Belong

Earlier this week as I was walking down my local main street, I was jolted out of a daydreaming reverie by a man cursing as he overtook me at a rapid pace. His head down, hands clenched, he looked up periodically at the shops as he passed, directing an aggressive but unclear message to them all. As he turned down the corner ahead of me, a woman walking in the opposite direction called out to him emphatically, 'You're upset because you think you don't belong!' It seemed a strange thing to call out, and I wondered if she knew him. When we caught up to each other she looked at me and repeated, 'He's upset because he thinks he doesn't belong'.

Not knowing quite what to say I asked naively, 'He thinks he doesn't belong in this suburb?'

'No. Anywhere!' she replied. I realised then that she didn't know the man, but wasn't a stranger to his experience.

'Oh. I think we all feel like that, sometimes', I said.

'Yes'. The woman looked at me intently. 'I went through it, but you get over it'.

At that moment a friend met up with her, and they walked off together as she started relaying what had happened.

I don't know if the woman's assumption about this particular man was correct, but its underlying premise struck me: we often act out aggressively when we feel rejected or excluded. A sense of belonging is a strong human need and for many it can be a long time coming. Indeed, the need to feel connected, to feel welcome, is so important to our sense of security that it can lead us to compromise our growth and self-expression as we try to fit in. Psychologist Abraham Maslow used the term 'Jonah Complex' to describe a fear of expressing our best talents; of 'giving voice' to our interests, our personality, who we are. 'What a man can be, he must be', said Maslow, and he called this need 'self-actualization'.

Maslow's 'Jonah Complex' refers to the Biblical prophet Jonah, who attempted to flee the mission God had given him (to warn a town of its wicked ways). Jonah covered his ears and ran away. Likewise, we can close our eyes and ears to the suggestion of new challenges or situations that could lead us to a greater embodiment of our personality: we can evade our destiny by holding ourselves back. For example, we may have a forte — parenting, or running a household or business; athletics, art, music, plumbing… It doesn't matter what it is that we do, just that it feels right: we enjoy it, there is something of 'us' about it, and we let ourselves excel (express ourselves fully) without fear of reprisal or rejection.

We often fear opportunities to express our talents or authentic self because we want to fit in with the crowd. We want to avoid punishment from society, or a particular group or person, so instead of standing out as something special we become pleasing and appeasing. We throw away possibilities, rein ourselves in, or put our hand down for the sake of security and belonging. We don't want to stick our head above the parapet.

The life of Nathan Cavaleri is a striking example of this. Cavaleri rose to fame in the 1990s as a child prodigy blues guitarist. When he was nine years old, he toured with Australian rock star Jimmy Barnes. At the same time as his career as a guitarist was taking off, Cavaleri was undergoing treatment for leukaemia. In an interview (*Australian Story*, ABC Television, 2019) Cavaleri spoke of how playing the guitar wasn't just a natural pleasure for him, it was a means of momentarily freeing him from the stress and pain of his treatment.

Cavaleri became a household name in Australia, appearing weekly on a television entertainment programme, and when he was given the all-clear when he was twelve, he toured the US, playing in blues clubs and appearing on popular talk shows. Cavaleri's star was on the rise; he jammed with guitar legends Aaron Neville, Robben Ford, went on tour with BB King for a whole summer, was signed to Michael Jackson's label and released a record in the States.

Upon return to Australia, Cavaleri's outstanding entry into the music world made him a target of bullies at high school. On the first day of term, a boy walked up to him, tripped him up, slammed a tennis ball into his eye, shouted profanities at him, and laughed before running off. Cavaleri stood out because of his fame, talent, and love of blues, but by the time he was fourteen, he had become embarrassed about his accomplishments. He refused to play the guitar at school, gave up music, and became a bricklayer's labourer upon graduation.

Mid-Life: Listening to the Call

In the first half of life, we try to deal with fears of abandonment and attack by holding back essential aspects of ourselves: we behave in ways that aren't really 'us', or at least, aren't *fully* us. We compromise; we try and deal with the fear of not belonging by acting compliantly or blending in. Sooner or later, however, our repressed aspects will call for expression, and this can cause significant anxiety, depression and fatigue.

Returning to Cavaleri, his love of music led him to form a band with friends which provided an outlet for his talent, albeit a limited one: the band played heavy rock music, and they didn't perform under the 'Nathan Cavaleri' banner. Cavaleri was afraid people would hate him or cringe when they heard his name — he was that kid who was all over the television in the nineties. The band was effectively a cover for his past, his prodigious talent and his appreciation for blues. The call to be himself caught up with him one day when he had a panic attack on stage. From that day forward he suffered acute anxiety at gigs and nearly blacked out on more than one occasion. The stage used to be Cavaleri's happy place, somewhere he felt comfortable, but the idea of touring came to terrify him.

Cavaleri stopped performing altogether as his anxiety and insomnia took over. He sought help from therapy and several other avenues, and three years later guitarist Kenny Jewell invited him to play at his weekly pub gig in Sydney. Cavaleri agreed, as it would be just the two of them on stage playing the blues, and Jewell wouldn't announce Cavaleri's name to the crowd. When Cavaleri took to the stage and began playing, his fear turned to excitement: he loved this kind of performance, it reminded him of how he used to play as a child. He also had an appreciative audience; he'd 'come home' to where he'd always belonged.

The performance ushered in a rebirth of Cavaleri's career and growth in self-acceptance. He realised he didn't need to underplay his achievements, that it was okay to be who he was. He was redeeming his true self and with this came a spark that had been missing for several years. But nothing was wasted. As Cavaleri told *Australian Story*, 'What I've learned over this whole period is how adversity can teach us and inspire growth. I think when I was a kid, I had something to play. But now I feel like I've got something to say'.

Embracing our authentic self is a step along the road to accepting our true, spiritual Self, because it involves forgiveness. In Cavaleri's case, he could always point a finger towards the bullies who teased him as a cause for unhappiness in the present — for feeling bad about his name, his talent, and his love of blues. By unashamedly expressing his talent and preferences, he was allowing his grievances to occupy a less prominent place in his mind. In effect, by reclaiming his true 'happy place', he was saying that the bullies hadn't done any lasting damage. He could be happy. He could feel fulfilled.

Form and Content

I love the phrase Cavaleri used to describe his transition from child musician to adult performer — from 'having something to play, to having something to say'. Using terminology from *A Course in Miracles*, we could say that the change in emphasis was from 'form to content'. Cavaleri's performance became less about technical display and more about communication. Through his trials and tribulations, Cavaleri had found his voice. Because this path involves confronting self-doubt, shame and guilt, we develop empathy along the way, and it is this relatedness that others connect with.

In line with this 'form/content' distinction, Patti Smith, the iconic poet, singer and songwriter from New York, talks about becoming less focused on technical proficiency while becoming more 'emphatically expansive' with age (*Q Magazine*, 2017). Likewise, in a talk-show interview with Norwegian journalist Fredrik Skavlan, Smith was asked if she'd call herself a perfectionist. 'No', she replied. There's a particular standard she likes to work to when creating something, but the most important thing for her when she's performing is communication: she doesn't mind if she makes a mistake or looks foolish as long as she feels that she and the audience are staying in tune with each other.

The irony of Smith's answer wasn't lost on Skavlan who then asked her about her performance in Stockholm at the 2016 Nobel Prize awards. 'That experience was the most difficult of my performing life', said Smith. Bob Dylan had been awarded the Nobel Prize in Literature and Patti Smith had been asked to sing in honour of the prize. In her essay, 'How Does It Feel', (*The New Yorker*, December 2016), Smith describes how she stood amongst the orchestra on the balcony of the Stockholm Concert Hall, overlooking the audience, which included the Swedish King and Queen and laureates past and present. After a speech in honour of Dylan was read, she heard her name called then started singing 'A Hard Rain's a-Gonna Fall'. She describes the first verse as 'passable, a bit shaky', but was confident she would settle. Instead, however, she became overwhelmed with emotion and froze during the second verse.

This was a novel experience for Smith, who wasn't accustomed to nerves during a performance. On this occasion, however, all she could do was stop singing. In her interview with Skavlan she described so ashamed that she covered her face. She asked the orchestra to stop and decided to just tell the truth. 'I'm sorry. I'm so nervous', she said. The audience was forgiving and applauded in encouragement as Smith asked the orchestra to backtrack so she could try again. As she recommenced singing, she could feel everyone with her, willing her on, and she completed the performance with a few minor stumbles but 'a lot of love in the room'. Some people were in tears.

In her essay, Smith wrote, 'As I took my seat, I felt the humiliating sting of failure, but also the strange realization that I had somehow entered and truly lived the world of the lyrics'. The song is, after all, about hard times; 'stumbling on the side of misty mountains', 'crawling on crooked highways'. Though Smith felt the dissatisfaction of not having 'nailed' the performance on one level, she was reassured the next day that it had been perfect:

> When I arose the next morning, it was snowing. In the breakfast room, I was greeted by many of the Nobel scientists. They showed appreciation for my very public struggle. They told me I did a good job. I wish I would have done better, I said. No, no, they replied, none of us wish that. For us, your performance seemed a metaphor for our own struggles. Words of kindness continued through the day, and in the end I had to come to terms with the truer nature of my duty. Why do we commit our work? Why do we perform? It is above all for the entertainment and transformation of the people. It is all for them. The song asked for nothing. The creator of the song asked for nothing. So why should I ask for anything?

A Course in Miracles, Kinship and Sameness

Echoing Smith's reflection on why she, as an artist, performs, the Course tells us that the most important question we can ask in a situation is 'What is it for?'

> In any situation in which you are uncertain, the first thing to consider, very simply, is 'What do I want to come of this? What is it for?' The clarification of the goal belongs at the beginning, for it is this which will determine the outcome.[23]

In terms of the Course, there are only two purposes, reflecting either a choice for the right mind or the wrong mind. If we choose to identify with the ego's wrong-minded thought system, our emphasis will be on reinforcing the belief in separation, which will be reflected in perceptions of superiority or inferiority, winners and losers, of feeling proud or deflated. The ego always gives to get because it doesn't identify with the abundance of Everything, and is full of self-doubt. In contrast, if we choose to identify with the Holy Spirit and the right-minded thought system, our emphasis will be on sharing; on what we give or extend rather than what we get back.

An experience of kinship, then, can come through failure of form. Patti Smith, carrying on despite her setbacks, is all of us carrying on despite our struggles with form. 'Why do we commit our work?' 'It is all for them.' 'Why should I ask for anything?' asks Smith. Love asks for nothing. If our goal is to share in an experience of kinship, then we have joined the Holy Spirit in one intent, and this is healing. In contrast, an emphasis on form at the expense of content means we are trying to triumph, and we are doing things on our own.

When we identify with the ego, we experience intense emotional needs, or 'neediness'. We have a need to triumph, a need for approval. In these moments, we are indeed only human. Smith's Nobel Prize performance could have turned out very differently. Initially, she felt ashamed, but then she chose not to focus on the form. The content was there and she carried on, and people joined with that and appreciated it. Smith was able to do this because she is well practiced at making kinship her main focus.

Reading Smith's memoir, *M Train*, I was struck by the focus on kinship at the heart of her travels — it's what motivates her. Smith continually seeks to connect with the inner experience of others, and I was particularly moved by her story of a trip to the late artist Frida Kahlo's house in Mexico. Smith had been asked to give a talk on Kahlo's life and work, and the day before the talk she became very ill with nausea and a migraine. The following morning, she felt well enough to fulfil her arrangement at Kahlo's residence-turned-museum, Casa Azul.

After arriving early to take some photographs (Smith is a keen photographer), Smith again felt sick and faint. The director of the museum insisted that she rest in one of the bedrooms. She lay down and fell asleep until the director woke her as the public were beginning to arrive. As the day turned to evening and two hundred guests were seated in the garden, Smith sang a song to them that had come to her while she'd been lying down — a song about the mounted butterflies that had been given to Kahlo by a friend during Kahlo's convalescence after losing a leg in a road accident. The butterflies hung in the bedroom so Kahlo could look at them from her bed.

Several people in the audience cried as Smith sung the butterfly song. Smith's suffering had served a greater purpose, just as it had in her Nobel Prize performance — it had prompted her to seek connection. She could have gone down a different road — lying sick on the bed she could have thought that the trip wasn't worth the trouble, that she wasn't being looked after well enough, or been resentful and critical of her illness. She could have felt at odds with the people around her, but this wasn't her goal, and so her experience was different:

> The value of deciding in advance what you want to happen is simply that you will perceive the situation as a means to make it happen. You will therefore make every effort to overlook what interferes with the accomplishment of your objective, and concentrate on everything that helps you meet it... The true becomes what can be used to meet the goal. The false becomes the useless from this point of view.[24]

The Course tells us that we are never healed alone, and that teaching and learning are the same. Smith taught kinship to her audiences and learnt kinship at the same time. Those in the audience with the same goal taught and learnt likewise.

Resistance

Maslow defined the Jonah Complex as a fear of being all you can be in terms of your personality or authentic self. But there's another way of looking at the Jonah Complex. In light of the Course, we can see it as the fear of unity, of experiencing kinship or joining. Underlying our fear of abandonment and attack is an investment in perceiving them because this reinforces the belief in our identity as a separate, ego self. You could say that the second half of life is where we realise that every problem — or everything we experience as a problem — has its roots in believing we are separate from God. Every time we reject God's Love, we fear his retaliation and rejection in turn. We project these fears out of our mind and onto the world where we anticipate retaliation and abandonment from others:

> All who believe in separation have a basic fear of retaliation and abandonment. They believe in attack and rejection, so that is what they perceive and teach and learn.[25]

Yet, we are attracted to feeling rejected and unfairly treated because this keeps our separate, individual 'I' front and centre: both pain and pleasure root our awareness to the body. Many psychologists talk about the 'toxicity' of shame, and counter it with statements such as 'you are worthy'. We are, however, resistant to feeling worthy because worthiness and holiness are synonymous. We don't want to be a holy spiritual Self in which we're united with everyone else, but a shameful, guilty, separate ego self. We want to remain self-centred instead of God-centred, and to do that we have to experience ourselves as better or worse than others — it doesn't matter which: being different is the main attraction.

It's virtually impossible in this world not to feel rejected, unfairly treated or to experience stress related to how we are treated and our circumstances. Nor is it helpful to try and deny these feelings. There comes a time, however, when we feel willing and able to move on. We can certainly be victimised, but we don't have to remain feeling hurt or robbed of peace forever — we accept that there is room for healing and transformation.

Whenever we feel rejected or unfairly treated, we can remember that we don't *have to* continue feeling that way. This is the beginning of healing. We can then ask the Holy Spirit's help to recognise our neighbour's need as our own. Forgiveness says, 'You can't affect my wholeness', which in turn sends the message that *neither of us* have ever hurt God. This is our only need — to know of our innocent, whole Self — and as we recognise this, we grow into who we are to be, free to use our voice, unafraid of 'making waves'. With the goal of remembering kinship in mind, we can wholeheartedly pursue an ideal in our own way.

Dream Worlds

The idea that the world is a dream, or an illusion, is not unique to *A Course in Miracles*. According to the Hindu Advaita philosophy, for example, Brahman (God) alone is real and the world is a dream of multiplicity that obscures the truth and reality of Oneness.

A Course in Miracles likewise describes the world as a dream, but it's a dream within a dream: there are two dreams at the heart of the Course's metaphysics, and this makes all the difference.

Dream Number One: The Secret Dream

The creation story at the centre of the Course's metaphysics begins with the idea that a part of Oneness experienced itself as separate from — different to — the rest of Oneness. Another way of saying this is that a part of an undifferentiated unity became *self*-conscious. This is clearly impossible, which leads to the question: How could the impossible happen? The Course's answer is that it didn't. This is the central teaching of the Course, and is the essence of its Atonement Principle which is that the separation from God never occurred, and so we have nothing to atone for — no need to feel unhappy, unloved or unlovable.

So how do we explain our experience in the world, as a separate, physical being? The Course says it is *as if* we fell asleep and dreamed a dream in which we could be different from our Source, a thing apart from Everything. This experience of separation was the beginning of the ego thought system and, dreaming we were separate, we wanted two things: to be the boss, and to be noticed as something special by God. Since God couldn't possibly notice anything as 'special' — as separate and different — we turned our back on His Love, in effect relegating an awareness of Oneness to the scrapheap, and setting ourselves up as an autonomous individual; 'the boss of us'.

Imagining ourselves to be a separate entity, we projected our own need for special recognition and dominance onto God, making Him into our own image. The ego's God demands veneration, divides us into sinners and saints, and is determined to punish us for usurping His authority. We also imagine that God has rejected us as something unworthy of his Love, kicking us out of Heaven, rather than it being *we* who abandoned *Him*. The idea that God is capable of attack (abandonment and retaliation) is what the Course calls 'the first projection of error outward':

> You who believe that God is fear made but one substitution. It has taken many forms, because it was the substitution of illusion for truth; of fragmentation for wholeness… That one error, which brought truth to illusion, infinity to time, and life to death, was all you ever made.[26]

This first dream is one of sin (I offended God), guilt (I'm bad), shame (I'm inferior), and fear (I'm going to get what's coming to me, and I'm going to be abandoned).

Dream Number Two: The World

Terrified of our fate at the hands of God's wrath, we escape the conflict within our mind by projecting the thought of separation outward, giving rise to a world of differences and competing interests; a world that is the opposite of Heaven's Oneness. In particular, where Heaven is a state of Love, the world is a screen onto which we project our separation fears:

> The dreaming of the world is… started by your secret dream, which you do not perceive although it caused the part you see and do not doubt is real. How could you doubt it while you lie asleep, and dream in secret that its cause is real?[27]

As long as we believe in the reality of separation from God, we'll perceive things in a way that justifies fear and feelings of unworthiness. And just as we projected the dream of separation and conflict onto the world, we project the guilt and shame associated with it onto others in another attempt to rid ourselves of fear.

According to the Course, every problem — everything we experience as a problem — has its roots in the drama of separation between ourselves and God — the sum and substance of the secret dream. The way we address this secret dream of conflict is to see how its themes are reflected in the world and notice our reactions. The 'God versus defiant child' scenario, for example, plays out in every facet of life. We see it in relations between parents and children, partners, and between leaders of any description and their followers. Even a computer that doesn't give you what you want is a handy screen for 'authority issues'. Abandonment, betrayal, unfair treatment: it's all the stuff of the secret dream.

Awakening and The Happy Dream

While our fears in the world seem bad enough, they are nothing compared to the terror we experienced in the first dream. We remain focused on the world as the source of pleasure and pain because on some level we know there is something we fear more, deep within the recesses of our mind, and we don't want to face it. Looking at it, however, is the only way we can bridge the gap between our false ego self and our true spiritual Self. Until we do so, we are at an impasse.

So, what do we do? Fortunately, the Course provides a means of awakening us gently from the dream of separation. We don't have to resign ourselves to the devil we know for fear of losing it to a terrifying fate. Instead, we leave the fearful dream of the world by exchanging it for a 'happy dream', a 'gentler dream' in which our suffering is healed and our neighbour is our friend.[28] This is the key to experiencing the Course's happy dream: we see 'our neighbour as our friend', a companion with the same self-doubt born of a belief in separation, the same spiritual Self, and the same need to finally feel at home.

The first step in awakening from the fearful dream of the world, of perceiving kinship instead of competition, is to realise we have a choice in how we perceive what is going on around us, and that it is *this decision* that determines our inner experience. If we choose to identify with the ego, we will perceive things in a way that has us seeing 'good' and 'bad' and taking sides. If we choose to identify with the Holy Spirit, we will see only calls for help or expressions of love, no matter the form of someone's behaviour.

It's in working with our perceptions of others that we undo the first projection of error; the belief that God is fear. We learn that God is Love by undoing our guilt, projected onto others. This is the indirect means the Course provides for approaching our fear of God.

> The face of Christ has to be seen before the memory of God can return.[29]

'Christ' in the Course refers to our spiritual Self; a complete and completely innocent Self. We see the face of Christ in everyone by acknowledging our sameness — our shared interests — as this is the earthly reflection of recognising the oneness of the Self. This leads to the happy dream in which we no longer shoulder a burden of guilt and shame, knowing that the nightmare of the secret dream is untrue. We don't take our egos or the egos of others seriously anymore: we know that when we get lost in concerns about worldly security, or feelings of competitiveness or unfair treatment, we've simply chosen to believe in the reality of the secret dream. When we're in the happy dream, we know that despite what goes on around us, despite our dualistic ('one or the other') thoughts, everything is fundamentally okay; 'not one note in Heaven's song was missed'.[30]

Workbook Lesson 155, 'I will step back and let Him lead the way', provides a lovely description of what it's like to be in the happy dream:

> There is a way of living in the world that is not here, although it seems to be. You do not change appearance, though you smile more frequently. Your forehead is serene; your eyes are quiet.[31]

We are still asleep, we still have an 'I', but that 'I' now moves backstage, letting the love of our Self lead the way. Through practicing forgiveness, we have arrived at 'the lawns of Heaven', where we wait patiently for God to take the final step, and eternity joins with us.

The Art of Listening

There is a vast number of therapies to help us move past hurts, fears, anxiety and depression. Each has their own take on what ails and what heals us, but I think all would agree that a capacity for listening is essential to an effective therapeutic process. Indeed, what sets Freud's psychoanalytic therapy apart from others is its emphasis on the type of listening the therapist should employ. In psychoanalysis, listening is an art; something that comes from deep within. In Freud's tradition, the art of listening *is* the art of healing.

How many times have you found yourself frowning while you're listening to someone talk? You don't necessarily disagree with them, or dislike what they're saying, but you're focused on trying to hold on to all the facts, on understanding. Listening in this way is a lot of work. 'It's exhausting talking to people all day': this is a common thread around the holiday season. And it's true. There can be lots of 'brain muscle' involved in everyday conversations.

The type of listening Freud insists on for therapy relates to his two fundamental rules of psychoanalysis. The first rule concerns free association, which is where the patient is to say whatever comes into their mind without censoring themselves. This is why the patient lies on a couch — the idea being that they'll be more relaxed, less guarded, and therefore more able to suspend the influence of their conscious, rational mind. In his essay, 'On Beginning the Treatment', Freud describes what the therapist could say to the patient at the start of their first session:

> What you tell me must differ in one respect from an ordinary

conversation. Ordinarily you rightly try to keep a connecting thread through your remarks and you exclude any intrusive ideas that may occur to you as side-issues, so as not to wander too far from the point. But in this case you must proceed differently... You will be tempted to say to yourself that this or that is irrelevant here, or quite unimportant, or nonsensical, so that there is no need to say it. You must never give in to these criticisms, but say it in spite of them...

Without censorship, repressed conflicts within the patient's unconscious are freer to emerge during free association, albeit often in a disguised, or symbolic, form.

The second fundamental rule relates to the therapist. In listening to the patient, the therapist must employ 'evenly-suspended attention' regarding everything they hear. This is one way, Freud says, that they can avoid burn-out or a strain on their attention from hours of work. But the more important by-product of this rule is that the therapist avoids 'deliberate attention'. As Freud described in 'Recommendations to Physicians Practicing Psychoanalysis':

For as soon as anyone deliberately concentrates his attention to a certain degree, he begins to select from the material before him; one point will be fixed in his mind with particular clearness and some other will be correspondingly disregarded, and in making this selection he will be following his expectations or inclinations...

With 'deliberate attention', the therapist's expectations will cause them to hone in on things that reinforce what they think they already know, and they'll disregard hunches that might well be true. In other words, with deliberate attention we become prematurely selective: 'It must not be forgotten', says Freud, 'that the things one hears are for the most part things whose meaning is only recognised later on'.

So, just as the patient is to speak freely without judging some things as worthy of expression and others unworthy, the therapist is to listen unselectively to what is said, and not try to keep anything particular in mind. The idea is that by putting their rational thought processes aside, the therapist allows their unconscious to respond to what they are hearing. This, according to Freud, is important because the therapist can only recognise the unconscious material concealed in what the patient says by using his or her own unconscious to first 'translate' it.

Freud's idea is that the therapist turns their unconscious like a microphone receiver towards the patient's unconscious: just as the electrical impulses down a telephone line are converted back to words and sounds by the receiver, the therapist's unconscious is able to reconstruct the patient's unconscious from the words spoken in free association. In relation to understanding the messages of the unconscious, you could say 'it takes one to know one'.

As the analyst responds from their unconscious, it's important that they don't censor their thoughts or inspirations, which can appear strange or irrelevant. A striking example of the sometimes 'out of the box' nature of prompts from the unconscious can be found in *C.G. Jung Speaking: Interviews and Encounters*. Here, Jung describes a session with a woman suffering from insomnia. Early in the session, Jung tries to emphasise the importance of relaxation to his patient:

> I tried to explain to her that relaxation was necessary, that I, for example, found relaxation by sailing on the lake, by letting myself go with the wind; that this was good for one, necessary for everybody. But I could see by her eyes that she didn't understand.
>
> She got it intellectually, that's as far as it went, though. Reason had no effect.

Jung's consciousness shifted gears as he talked about sailing and the wind, and he heard the voice of his mother singing a lullaby about a little girl in a boat: 'And I began, almost without doing it on purpose, to hum what I was telling her about the wind, the waves, the sailing, and relaxation, to the tune of the little lullaby.'

Jung's patient was transfixed by the song, and later found that her insomnia had disappeared. Using Freud's microphone receiver analogy, Jung turned his unconscious mind towards the client to receive the messages from her unconscious and translate them, providing a response from his own unconscious that spoke to the needs expressed.

Listening with the Holy Spirit

I'm sure Jung would have little trouble with the microphone receiver analogy — the idea of one unconscious recognising the symbols and meanings of another. A major difference between him and Freud, however, is that Jung attributed wisdom to the unconscious. For Jung, maintaining 'evenly-suspended attention' when listening wasn't about tuning in to an organic decoding machine, but to something that had healing and wholeness as its goal. This 'something' is the wisdom of the unconscious, a spiritual aspect of the mind, which for Jung meant it transcended the ego and the limits of rationality.

Jung's definition of 'spiritual' isn't directly translatable as the 'spiritual' of religions, as something otherworldly per se. It is still based on the phenomenology of the mind, but it relates to a 'higher consciousness', a source of insight that is beyond our personal 'I' (see, for example, 'Spirit and Life', *Collected Works: Volume 8*). Jung's work has often been misunderstood because of the distinctive meaning he gives to traditionally religious terms and symbology.

Suffice to say, that while Jung attributed a source of wisdom to the unconscious that was beyond the 'I, me and mine' associated with a biological creature trying to avoiding pain and experience pleasure, Freud did not. In Freud's view, the benefit of the therapist's prompts from tuning in to their unconscious and deciphering the patient's 'transmissions', is that they can help unblock the free association process: as the therapist's questioning or suggestions help move things along, the gradual telling of the patient's story unfolds, and this is central to healing. In Jung's system, there is also the possibility that prompts from the unconscious can function as healing agents in and of themselves. When the doctor of Jung's insomnia patient met him at a conference, he asked Jung what he had done to cure her — surely he hadn't sung her a lullaby as she had reported:

> How was I to explain to him that I had simply listened to something within myself? I had been quite at sea. How was I to tell him that I had sung her a lullaby with my mother's voice? Enchantment like that is the oldest form of medicine. But it all happened outside of my reason: it was not until later that I thought about it rationally and tried to arrive at the laws behind it. She was cured by the grace of God.

Over the door at Jung's house in Zurich, he had inscribed in Latin: 'Whether summoned or not, God will be present', yet we have no clear Jungian definition of 'God'. To Jung, God was something mysterious and incomprehensible that inspired our spiritual yearning; our desire for meaning and purpose. God's Will, or Grace, could move through us towards spiritual growth, and for Jung such growth meant individuation. To be 'individuated' is to be undivided; our total self; who we are. Until then, we repress certain aspects due to shame and guilt, and project them onto others, either judging them harshly or becoming spellbound in adoration. The individuation process is simply one of letting ourselves grow to our fullest; like an acorn into an oak. This, for Jung, was a spiritual quest, one in line with the will of God.

The individuation process itself requires developing a receptivity to something beyond the rationality, planning and defensiveness of our ego. I like how Joseph Campbell put it in *Pathways to Bliss*: 'Make your god transparent to the transcendent, and it doesn't matter what his name is'. We must make ourselves 'transparent to the transcendent' by employing a kind of listening, making ourselves receptive to inner promptings that might go against the grain of external expectations or the advice and values of society. This enables us to live a truly creative life, born anew on a daily basis.

In terms of *A Course in Miracles*, we could say that by listening to his patient with his unconscious, Jung connected with a symbol — the lullaby — that conveyed 'the grace of God', the Holy Spirit's message. This message contained the memory of the patient's spiritual Self along with the reassurance that everything is okay — that she could relax. This is, in essence, the message of the Atonement: that the separation from God never occurred, everything is okay, we are at Home in God. And, in giving Jung his due, we could also say that the patient's healing would be reflected in her coming more 'into her own', letting go of some aspect of her past and further embodying the wholeness of her personality: the acorn into the oak.

An emphasis on quieting the ego's 'raucous shrieking' in order to listen to the Holy Spirit is a major theme in the Course. The shrieking of our ego is all about neediness: needing to be right, to be heard, to be approved of, to be preferred. We can't truly listen as long as our neediness is operating. If we're not relaxed, we're not listening; not with the Holy Spirit, anyway. The way to listen with the Holy Spirit is to notice when we're *not* listening with Him. We notice when we're judging someone, when we've become agitated or impatient, fixed on an idea, or determined to be right. As we ask for help to remember our shared need — to know of the innocence and wholeness of our spiritual Self — we both gain. *Your problem is the same as my problem.* When we remember this, judgment is replaced by an 'evenly-suspended attention', listening begins, and healing occurs.

The Split—Part I: Freud, Jung and the Oceanic Feeling

In the preface of *A Course in Miracles*, Helen Schucman (the Course's scribe) describes how the Course came about:

> A Course in Miracles began with the sudden decision of two people to join in a common goal. Their names were Helen Schucman and Bill Thetford... It represented a truly collaborative venture between Bill and myself, and much of its significance, I am sure, lies in that. I would take down what the Voice 'said' and read it to him the next day, and he typed it from my dictation.

Helen and Bill were opposites in many regards. They had different temperaments and clashed on a regular basis. In their differences, however, they also found support. Where Helen was of the Freudian school and 'atheistic in belief', Bill was open to ideas about transcendence, mysticism, and Eastern philosophies. It was Bill's knowledge in such areas that helped Helen come to terms with scribing the Course, providing some context for it and mitigating her fear of the process.

In previous posts (see *Reflections on* A Course in Miracles, Volume Three), I've explored the Freudian and Jungian aspects of the Course. Though Helen did open her mind to the idea and experience of spiritual transcendence,

Freud would not, and this was a major factor in his split with Jung. The following discussion explores Freud's resistance, and though it doesn't address *A Course in Miracles* directly, we might gain some insight into why we too might resist transcendence.

Sigmund Freud and Carl Jung met in 1907 following a written correspondence in which Jung sent Freud his *Studies in Word Association*. That first encounter was a powerful meeting of minds; the two talked for over twelve hours straight. The next six years marked a time of intense collaboration, but in 1913 it all came to an end — the relationship was no longer amicable.

A major factor in the split was Jung's refusal to compromise his ideas about religion in order to bring them in line with Freud's libido theory. Libido, said Freud, is an instinctual drive for sexual pleasure, and is a fundamental motivator. We experience significant inner tension when our libido clashes with the rules and expectations of society. 'The only way to get rid of a temptation is to yield to it. Resist it, and your soul grows sick with longing for the things it has forbidden to itself', Oscar Wilde wrote in his novel *The Picture of Dorian Gray*. This depicts the Freudian dilemma: how to manage our desires in a way that is acceptable within society and at the same time leads to some satisfaction?

Freud's concept of libido follows from philosopher Arthur Schopenhauer's idea of 'the will', our inner nature consisting of a blind ceaseless striving — the irrational drives of a biological creature, embodied in flesh and bone. Like Schopenhauer, Freud imagined the libido to be something associated with our experience as a biological entity, nothing more. He believed it was a substance circulating throughout the body influencing the nervous system, in turn causing our psychological movements towards and away from things — our desires and aversions.

Jung's concept of libido is broader than Freud's. To Jung, libido is vital psychic energy that motivates a person in various ways, including spiritually, intellectually and creatively. A person's psychological motivation can't always be reduced to a biological imperative. On the issue of art, for example,

Jung disagreed with Freud's view that all art is sexual expression, albeit in a sublimated form. Indeed, the central role of sexuality in Freud's system was never accepted by Jung. Jung therefore refused to explain religion and spirituality purely in terms of Freud's libido theory.

This chapter looks at Freud's answer to his quest for a libido-religion connection, and why he was so resistant to the idea of spiritual transcendence. The discussion is divided into two parts. In Part One, we'll explore connections between Freud's view of religion, women, mystical experience and intuition. In Part Two we'll address his resistance to an in-depth contemplation of transcendence, focusing on his unique childhood experience within a complicated family network. We'll also contrast his views on religion with Jung's, taking into account the influence of their different childhood experiences.

But first, let's take a look at Freud's revealing correspondence with a person who was no stranger to transcendent experience, the very thing Freud found so problematic.

Freud and Rolland: The Odd Couple

Freud is most famous for his theory on the psychosexual stages of development. You might be familiar with the unflattering term 'anal retentive', or simply 'anal', depicting a person who is fastidious, extremely orderly, for whom everything has to be 'just right'. The term is a product of Freud's psychosexual theory and refers to the anal stage of development when we begin toilet training. If a child experiences conflict around toilet training — issues of compliance or rebellion, control or shame — they can develop an 'anal retentive' character.

You might also be familiar with the term Oedipal Complex, which describes Freud's theory of what causes us the greatest angst. Most of our adult hang-ups, our triggers and hates, stem from this later, genital stage of development arising between the ages of three and five. This is when (according to Freud) we want to 'marry' one parent and kill off the other, who is now a love-rival.

We'll revisit this theory later in more detail, but at this stage it is sufficient to say that Freud's name is generally associated with sexuality and problems with authority figures, not with spiritual matters. But, as the following correspondence with French novelist and playwright Romain Rolland shows, Freud was still unsettled by (and therefore not totally resistant to) ideas related to spirituality, particularly towards the end of his life.

Freud was seventy-seven when he began writing to Rolland, expressing admiration for his work. Following the Great War, Freud seemed concerned for the future of society and humanity's fitness for civilisation. In Rolland, however, he observed an extraordinary character. Rolland had written articles during the war, calling for mutual respect and an end to hostilities, and was awarded The Nobel Prize in Literature 1915, 'as a tribute to the lofty idealism of his literary production and to the sympathy and love of truth with which he has described different types of human beings' (*Nobel Foundation Archive*, 1915).

While the younger Freud had never had a congenial conversation with Carl Jung over spiritual matters (Freud wasn't open to it at the time), with Rolland he shared a dialogue on the subject that was both detailed and respectful. The two disagreed, but they disagreed amicably, and their correspondence spurred Freud on to further musings captured in later works (most notably in *Civilisation and Its Discontents*).

In 1927 Freud sent Rolland a copy of his book *The Future of an Illusion*, in which he described the origin of religion as stemming from an infantile need for security in the world and a longing for the father-figure:

> Now when the child grows up and finds that he is destined to remain a child for ever, and that he can never do without protection against unknown and mighty powers, he invests these with the traits of the father-figure; he creates for himself the gods, of whom he is afraid, whom he seeks to propitiate, and to whom he nevertheless entrusts the task of protecting him.

Following his split from Jung in 1913, Freud had written *Totem and Taboo*, his own answer to the quest he had tried to give to Jung: to explain religion in terms of his libido theory. In his paper he explained the development of religion in terms of a social dynamic that emerged in humanity's distant past; a product of a 'coup d'état'. Freud's story starts with a 'primal horde' of brothers who were resentful of their father's power and claim to all of the women, and so banded together, killed him and ate his body, thereby 'acquiring a portion of his strength'.

Fearing punishment (the father more omnipresent in death than in life) and with reverence for his power, they created a totem — a symbol of the father — and worshipped it as father-substitute in the hope that this would appease him and elicit his protection. This primal horde narrative puts Freud's Oedipal theory at the heart of his conception of religious development.

Rolland didn't agree with Freud's theory that all religious sentiment could be explained by a regressive childhood desire for the protection of the father. Rolland had a strong interest in Eastern philosophy, particularly in the Vedanta of India. (He was writing biographies of Ramakrishna and Vivekananda — both Indian Hindu mystics — around the time of his correspondence with Freud.)

In 1929, Freud received the following letter from Rolland:

> Your analysis of religion is a just one. But I would have liked to see you doing an analysis of spontaneous religious sentiment or, more exactly, of religious feeling, which is wholly different from religion in the strict sense of the word, and much more durable.
>
> What I mean is: totally independent of all dogma, all credo, all Church organization, all Sacred Books, all hope in a personal survival, etc., the simple and direct fact of the feeling of the 'eternal' (which can very well not be eternal, but simply without perceptible limits, and like oceanic as it were)...
>
> I think that you will classify it also under the Zwangsneurosen [obsessional neuroses]. But I have often had occasion to observe its

rich and beneficent power, be it among the religious souls of the West, Christians or non-Christians, or among those great minds of Asia who have become familiar to me and some of whom I count as friends...

Rolland goes on to say that he has experienced this 'oceanic' feeling and it has nothing to do with wishful thinking (for a father substitute to help ensure his survival) but simply comes of its own accord:

> I may add that this 'oceanic' sentiment has nothing to do with my personal yearnings. Personally, I yearn for eternal rest, survival has no attraction for me at all. But the sentiment I experience is imposed on me as a fact. It is a contact. And as I have recognized it to be identical (with multiple nuances) in a large number of living souls, it has helped me to understand that that was the true subterranean source of religious energy which, subsequently, has been collected, canalized and dried up by the Churches...
>
> What eternal confusion is caused by words, of which the same one here sometimes means: allegiance to or faith in a dogma, or a word of god (or a tradition); and sometimes: a free vital upsurge.
>
> Please believe, dear friend, in my affectionate respect.
> Romain Rolland

Freud Digs In

The idea that a person could experience a feeling of oneness — a sense of all-inclusiveness — went contrary to everything Freud had taught about human nature. As such, he didn't revise his thoughts in a way that accommodated such transcendence. Instead, he explained the oceanic feeling in a way that fit into his long-standing biological appreciation of human nature. In other words, Freud reasoned that the oceanic consciousness must be a consequence of instinctual biological needs. In *Civilisation and Its Discontents,* Freud relates the oceanic feeling to a yearning for the experience of oneness in the womb, or the feeling of merging during sexual encounter.

Civilisation and Its Discontents is at least in part a reply to this letter from Rolland. It is one of Freud's major works and begins with a distinction between the majority of people who commonly seek power, success and wealth, and a minority 'whose greatness rests on qualities and achievements that are quite foreign to the aims and the ideals of the many'. One of these great men to which Freud refers is Rolland:

> One of these outstanding men corresponds with me and in his letters calls himself my friend. I sent him a little piece of mine that treats religion as an illusion, and in his reply he said that he wholly agreed with my view of religion, but regretted that I had failed to appreciate the real source of religiosity. This was a particular feeling of which he himself was never free, which he had found confirmed by many others and which he assumed was shared by millions, a feeling that he was inclined to call a sense of 'eternity', a feeling of something limitless, unbounded — as it were 'oceanic'. This feeling was a purely subjective fact, not an article of faith; no assurance of personal immortality attached to it, but it was the source of the religious energy that was seized upon by the various churches and religious systems, directed into particular channels and certainly consumed by them...
>
> This opinion of my esteemed friend... caused me no small difficulty. I can discover no trace of this 'oceanic' feeling in myself...

Freud goes on to say that his book is a way of: 'clearing it [the oceanic feeling issue] out of the way, so to speak'.

No one was going to sway Freud from his purely psychosexual conception of human beings, but we might wonder why a person so imaginative and broad in intellectual scope was so resistant to exploring the idea of human transcendence in any real depth. In relation to the oceanic feeling enigma, why was Freud so keen to 'clear it out of the way'? To begin this exploration, we need to consider Freud's thoughts on all things 'feminine'.

Freud, Women and Intuition

In line with his concept of religious aspiration, Jung's approach to wellbeing has a Yin–Yang quality missing in Freud's. This is because Freud's whole psychological framework rests on his Oedipal theory which, to put it bluntly, is phallocentric. According to Freud, there is no need for 'feminine and masculine' aspects of the psyche to achieve some kind of balance, or dialogue. Freud was steadfast in his belief that the sexual and genital-based scenario at the centre of his Oedipal theory meant that women and men develop a totally different psychological make-up; at least, that is the case if they have resolved the Oedipal Complex successfully.

One of Freud's most widely criticised papers is 1925's *The Psychological Consequences of the Anatomic Distinction Between the Sexes*. Here, Freud details the usual aspects of the Oedipal Complex — the son falls in love with his mother and fears punishment from his father. This essay, however, goes beyond his earlier works in that it focuses on the fact that boys and girls have different genitals, and therefore have a completely different Oedipal Complex. Boys, according to Freud, fall in love with their mother but don't fear their father until they notice that women don't have a penis. This realisation makes boys fearful of being castrated by the father: '... it arouses a terrible storm of emotion in him and forces him to believe in the reality of the threat he has hitherto laughed at'.

Having noticed that girls don't have a penis, the boy is either horrified or feels triumphant contempt for girls, but his fear of castration remains. To deal with this fear, he renounces his romantic feelings for his mother and identifies with his father (decides to become 'just like dad'), and that is how he resolves the Oedipus Complex. Girls, on the other hand, aware that they don't have a penis, conclude they have already been castrated. They feel inferior and develop 'penis envy'. In normal development, they eventually give up this wish, replacing it with a wish to have a child — a 'penis-child', as Freud labelled the symbolic substitution. And with the purpose of having a child in mind, the girl then develops romantic feelings for her father: 'Her mother becomes the object of her jealousy. The girl has turned into a little woman', and women, according to Freud, seek fulfilment.

And here is the crux of Freud's distinction between the sexes and his justification for the gender roles observed in his time. Boys, having had to renounce their desires for their mother because of their fear of castration, have a more highly developed super-ego (conscience) than women, and therefore higher ethical standards and a greater capacity to endure hardships. I'll let Freud dig his own grave here:

> Characteristics which critics of every epoch have brought up against women – that they show less sense of justice than men, that they are less ready to submit to the great exigencies of life, that they are more often influenced in their judgements by feelings of affection or hostility – all these would be amply accounted for by the modification in the formation of their super-ego which we have inferred above. We must not allow ourselves to be deflected from such conclusions by the denial of the feminists, who are anxious to force us to regard the two sexes as completely equal in position and worth.

Freud makes himself clear: the psychology of renunciation is superior to the psychology of fulfilment; men have claim to the former, and women to the latter.

Freud's Oedipus Complex theory, applied to the anatomical differences between the sexes, thus contributed to a theory of gender, and a neat explanation of the existing patriarchy. It normalised traditional, conservative gender roles by giving them the status of 'Oedipal Complex successfully worked through'. Those who strayed outside the norm — homosexuals, people who didn't want to have children, women who wanted to become doctors, men who weren't 'austere' — hadn't matured properly.

Freud's theory fitted neatly into the culture of the time: it 'explained' the current situation and justified maintaining the status quo. Likewise, society as it stood, aided and abetted Freud's satisfaction with his theory: society and Freud enjoyed a convenient positive feedback loop.

Psychoanalyst Karen Horney took issue with Freud's neat formulation. She suggested that Freud's theory of penis envy made more sense as a metaphor: women felt inferior because of their lack of social status and opportunities, not because of their literal lack of the phallus. She also coined the term 'womb envy', virtually saying to Freud, 'Two can play that game'. She introduced the idea that men could be affected by their inability to carry children, developing envy of the vital 'biological functions of the female sex' such as breastfeeding and pregnancy. You could, said Horney, see males striving for achievement as compensation for feelings of insignificance.

The point in all of this, is that Freud devalued all things stereotypically linked to the feminine. Not only was sensuality downplayed as a feminine trait, so too was intuition, mysticism and therefore, by association, the oceanic feeling. If Freud couldn't explain something according to his rationality, he regarded it as regressive or simply avoided it all together. Take, for instance, his relationship towards music; the most abstract of all the arts. In his paper *The Moses of Michelangelo*, Freud wrote:

> I am no connoisseur in art, but simply a layman... Nevertheless, works of art do exercise a powerful effect on me, especially those of literature and sculpture, less often of painting... I spend a long time before them trying to apprehend them in my own way, i.e., to explain to myself what their effect is due to. Wherever I cannot do this, as for instance with music, I am almost incapable of obtaining any pleasure. Some rationalistic, or perhaps analytic, turn of mind in me rebels against being moved by a thing without knowing why

I am thus affected and what it is that affects me.

An echo is found in reply to Rolland's letter about the oceanic feeling: 'How remote from me are the worlds in which you move! To me mysticism is just as closed a book as music'. Freud might have added women to this list of inaccessible phenomena: 'The great question that has never been answered, and which I have not yet been able to answer, despite thirty years of research into the feminine soul, is "What does a woman want?"' Perhaps Freud didn't understand women because he assumed their desires were so different to his own: his Oedipal theory demanded it.

Renunciation and Judaism

The issue of renunciation versus fulfilment also takes centre stage in Freud's analysis of what it means to be Jewish. Freud didn't share in the nationalistic ideals or the religion of his ancestors, but he still identified as Jewish; he still 'felt' Jewish. In the Hebrew translation of *Totem and Taboo*, Freud asks himself what it is that makes him identify as a Jew: what left of him is Jewish? 'A very great deal, and *probably its essence*', is his response, and *Moses and Monotheism* is his exploration of what that essence is.

Freud's paper starts with a retelling of the story in which Jews are led out of captivity in Egypt and Moses establishes a monotheistic religion. Compared with the polytheism of the Egyptian religion and its elaborate symbology and iconography, Judaism was austere. And so, following Freud's logic that austerity and renunciation of sensuality leads to a more developed intellect, Judaism (in Freud's view) 'forced upon the people an advance in intellectuality which, important enough in itself, opened the way, in addition, to... further renunciations of instinct'. The essence of being Jewish, for Freud, therefore lay in an elevation of intellectualism.

Freud's Judaism rejected the magic and mysticism of other religions, Christianity amongst them. Having developed out of Judaism, Christianity, according to Freud, wasn't strictly monotheistic because its doctrine of the

Trinity (The Father, Son and Holy Ghost), had a more sensual character in its use of symbolic rituals and iconography, and had 're-established the great mother-goddess' by way of its veneration for the Virgin Mary. A lot of what Freud said about women, he implied about Christianity (Catholicism in particular): it is more sensual than intellectual, it doesn't involve the renunciation and therefore engage the psychological strength of Judaism, it lacks critical reason; it is too emotional. And what dwells at the heart of the oceanic feeling but an emotional experience?

Cleary, Freud had built a strong case against entertaining the oceanic feeling as anything *but* a regressive experience based on a yearning for the womb, or the protective father, or a time in infancy when we didn't feel so vulnerable in the face of life's contingencies. Freud had built a fortress against 'the feminine', but in the true spirit of Freudian analysis we might ask, 'Why the need for such a strong barrier?' Was Freud afraid of something he wasn't aware of?

The Split—Part II: Freud, Jung and the Oceanic Feeling

I hope that Freud and his pupils will push their ideas to their utmost limits, so that we may learn what they are. They can't fail to throw light on human nature, but I confess that he made on me personally the impression of a man obsessed with fixed ideas.
— William James, letter to Theodore Flournoy, 1909

What he said about his sexual theory impressed me. Nevertheless, his words could not remove my hesitations and doubts. I tried to advance these reservations of mine on several occasions, but each time he would attribute them to my lack of experience... I could see that his sexual theory was enormously important to him, both personally and philosophically.
— Carl Jung, *Memories, Dreams, Reflections*

Freud was right when he said that women throughout the ages have been characterised in depreciating terms; patriarchy has reinforced the idea that women 'show less sense of justice than men' and are 'less ready to submit to the great exigencies of life'. Karen Horney (in *The Flight from Womanhood*) suggests that rather than such depreciation reflecting a truth, as Freud had assumed, it indicates an emotional need on the part of the depreciators:

> Further, we observe that men are evidently under a greater necessity to depreciate women than conversely... if there actually are in men tendencies to depreciate women behind this conviction of feminine inferiority, we must infer that this unconscious impulse to depreciation is a very powerful one.

And here we stand with Freud and his tendency to depreciate everything 'feminine'. Why did he need to do this? Freud's insistence on a universal sexual element to the Oedipal Complex holds a vital clue. Today, it's generally acknowledged that children commonly go through a stage of favouring one parent over another, acting out against the love-rival. The idea that sexual feelings are behind such favouritism isn't widely accepted, however Freud would turn in his grave if he knew his Oedipal theory had been divested of its sexual element. When Jung suggested to him that a child's desire for the exclusive love of their mother might relate to a longing for comfort — for the parent's sole attention and care — Freud wouldn't have it, and there are several probable reasons for this.

The Oedipal Complex arose from Freud's self-analysis after the death of his father. Freud was trying to solve the puzzle of his own neurotic symptoms: his anxieties, depression and psychosomatic complaints. Up to that point, his theory of 'hysterical neuroses' held that an adult's neurotic symptoms were due to a repressed memory of childhood sexual abuse; he called this his 'seduction theory' of neurosis. In his self-analysis, Freud was on the hunt for a memory of abuse at the hands of his father. He didn't, however, find one. Instead, through a series of dreams and memories, he realised that a significant event in his childhood was when he became aware of sexual feelings towards his mother. In a letter to his friend Wilhelm Fliess, he described how when he was about four or five years old, his 'libido towards *matreum* [mother] was awakened, namely on the occasion of a journey with her from Leipzig to Vienna...'

Freud saw parallels between his experience and the play *Oedipus Rex* by Sophocles, in which King Oedipus kills his father and marries his mother

— hence the 'Oedipus Complex'. In the letter to Fliess he writes, 'I have found, in my own case too, the phenomena of being in love with my mother and jealous of my father, and I now consider it a universal event in early childhood'.

Fliess was a huge influence on Freud. An ear, nose and throat specialist, Fliess was also interested in childhood sexuality, writing several papers which set the stage for Freud's Oedipal theory. Indeed, terms such as 'latency', 'sublimation', and 'reaction formation', which Freud used, came from Fliess, and in Fliess, Freud found support for his interpretation of his childhood experience. This interpretation led him to propose his psychosexual developmental model including the 'anal stage' and the subsequent 'genital stage' with its Oedipal Complex.

A major criticism of Freud's theory is that it largely ignores the influence of the parents' behaviour. Context is important. If a child gets fixated on erotic feelings towards a parent, it can be because of a breakdown in the relationship between the parents — the mother or father focuses on the child to get what they don't get from their partner emotionally. It's in such a scenario that the child becomes Oedipus, and Freud's relationship with his mother suggests that this was the case for himself.

Freud and Amalia

Freud's family make-up was anything but straightforward. His father Jacob had married twice previously, had two grown sons and was forty when he married twenty-year-old Amalia (Sigmund's mother). One of Freud's older half-brothers, Phillip, was close in age to Amalia, and to Freud seemed more of a 'companion' and better matched to her than was Jacob. Freud was also the same age as his other half-brother's son, his nephew John. Things must have been confusing.

Into this tangled web of relationships, Freud found himself the focus of his mother's worldly aspirations. This undoubtedly influenced his later Oedipal theory for girls which assumes they seek a 'penis-child' to make up for their feelings of inferiority. Better still, if that child is a boy, said Freud in *New*

THE SPLIT—PART II: FREUD, JUNG AND THE OCEANIC FEELING

Introductory Lectures on Psychoanalysis:

> A mother is only brought unlimited satisfaction by her relationship to her son; this is altogether the most perfect, most free from ambivalence of all human relationships. A mother can transfer to her son the ambition she has been obliged to suppress in herself, and she can expect from him the satisfaction of all that has been left over in her of her masculinity complex.

Freud was indisputably his mother's favourite. The oldest of seven children, Freud had been born 'en caul', which means he was still fully encased in the amniotic sack. This is a rare occurrence that happens once in every 80,000 births, and Freud's mother, Amalia, saw this as a sign that he was destined for fame. Adding to this was the prophecy of an old woman the young mother and son encountered in a pastry shop. Sigmund was destined for greatness, she had said. Sigmund's father merely had the presence of a 'benign old man' within the Freud household. Sigmund was the star to whom his mother attached herself.

He was her 'Golden Sigi', but Amalia was also a domineering figure. It was important to her that Sigmund become someone great, and her encouragement to this effect would undoubtedly have also been experienced as pressure.

Freud had his relationship with Amalia in mind when developing his Oedipal theory, however there is no detailed exploration of his feelings regarding the relationship, nor of his relationship with his father. His self-analysis stops as soon as he interprets his personal experience along 'natural', developmental lines; he distances himself from his experience by giving it a universal, 'par for the course', quality. He therefore doesn't have to go near the intolerable sensation of his mother's emotional domination.

Freud's thoughts in *Some Psychological Consequences of the Anatomical Distinction Between the Sexes* can be interpreted as his defence against his fear of female power, represented most potently for him in the figure of Amalia. It's interesting that Freud's most contentious commentary appears in his later works, in his sixties and seventies, around the period of his correspondence with Romain Rolland. As he doubles down against the reality of spiritual transcendence, so too does he ramp up his efforts to define the sexes in dichotomous and evaluative (superior/inferior) terms.

Freud dug himself into a hole by insisting on a sexual aspect to his Oedipal theory. His concept of castration anxiety led to the assumption of a fundamental difference between the psychologies of the sexes, and the value associated with each. To recap: boys, having had to renounce their incestuous desires out of fear of castration, have (according to Freud) a more developed conscience and are more directed by reason than women who are more susceptible to their feelings and sensuality. And since Freud sees reason and intellectualism as the foundation of civilised society and progress, the value of 'male psychology' over 'female psychology' is clear. To give value to the intuitive, emotional aspects within his own psyche would be to align himself with inferiority. Freud wouldn't have that. He was a man of critical reason and for whom professional and social status was important, and had emphasised the more progressive status of his race and gender by emphasising their superior intellect.

It Starts at Home: Jung the Transcendentalist

Just as Freud's Oedipus Complex is grounded in his childhood experience, Jung's theories relate to the context of his earliest years. In particular, Jung's openness to the idea of spiritual transcendence is understandable in light of experiences mentioned in his memoir *Memories, Dreams, Reflections*. Here he describes childhood visions, which evoked a numinous experience, or a feeling for the eternal, the transcendent; for mystery.

The son of a pastor, Jung went to church regularly. Though he hated going, and rebelled against the Church in his teens, he — like Romain Rolland — was able to make a distinction between Church doctrine and his inner experience of the transcendent, what he termed 'God'. His potent transcendent experiences in childhood were aided and abetted by his solitude at home. Where Freud was the eldest of seven children born in quick succession, and had his nephew as a steadfast playmate — a 'companion in his misdeeds' — Jung had no siblings until he was nine, when his sister was born. Where the Freud household was a hive of activity, the Jung household was a relatively quiet place where young Carl enjoyed the only kind of play available to him — the solitary kind:

> I played alone, and in my own way. Unfortunately I can't remember what I played; I recall only that I did not want to be disturbed. I was deeply absorbed in my games and could not endure being watched or judged while I played them… One of my reasons for liking school was that there I found at last the playmates I had lacked for so long.

Starting school, at age six, wasn't a straightforward experience for Jung. He noticed that when he was with his 'rustic schoolmates' he was different to how he was at home. He found that being with them alienated him from himself; at least, from the self he knew he was when he played alone, in a world that contained only his parents. This was the beginning of Jung's realisation of having a No. 1 Personality and a No. 2 Personality; a personality related to the outer world, and another related to the inner. The No. 1 Personality was all about getting by in the practical world: going to school, doing homework, making friends, carrying out responsibilities. The No. 2 Personality was the one capable of spiritual experiences.

Jung's appreciation for transcendence — for a layer of being that is not of this world — is clearly expressed in his work *Mysterium Coniunctionis*. Here he writes that our inner and outer worlds rest 'on a transcendental background' that we can't describe:

The existence of a transcendental reality is indeed evident in itself, but it is uncommonly difficult for our consciousness to construct intellectual models which would give a graphic description of the reality we have perceived. Our hypotheses are uncertain and groping, and nothing offers us the assurance that they may ultimately prove correct.

This transcendental background is particularly evident in meaningful coincidences, or instances of synchronicity. The striking thing in synchronicity is that something occurs in the external world which speaks directly to what is going on within our psyche. It is a meeting point of internal and external reality:

> Though we know from experience that psychic processes are related to material ones, we are not in a position to say in what this relationship consists or how it is possible at all. Precisely because the psychic and the physical are mutually dependent it has often been conjectured that they may be identical somewhere beyond our present experience...

There appears, said Jung, to be another dimension that transcends the world of form and linear time, and operates as an ordering principle according to the meaning, or equivalence, of things: moments of synchronicity can be seen as signposts that meets us in the psychological condition we find ourselves in, helping to guide us. This transcendent dimension exists outside time and space as we know it. Exactly how synchronicity actually happens was the subject of many discussions between Jung and the physicist Wolfgang Pauli, the two striking up a friendship that lasted over twenty years.

Another possible reason for Freud's resistance to contemplating transcendence is his belief in the Newtonian concept of linear time. This concept works well for considering a continuous chain of events, such as in his primal horde story, or stages of psychosexual development. This linear cause-effect approach mirrors Charles Darwin's evolutionary theory, which had inspired the young Freud to study biology and medicine. Where Freud was embedded in biology and the concept of linear time, Jung was fascinated by the relatively new science of quantum physics, which turned traditional concepts of time and space (and the distinction between subject and observer) on their head. It's hard to imagine Freud giving much thought to the existence of a space-time continuum or other mind-bending discoveries of modern physics. 'What does any of that have to do with castration anxiety?!' he might ask.

It Starts at Home: Jung the Alchemist

Freud's inner crisis and self-analysis after his father died led to his theory of the Oedipal Complex. Likewise, Jung experienced a lengthy Dark Night of the Soul following his split from Freud in 1913. His *Red Book* is a personal exploration of the depths of his unconscious during this period, a time in which he felt alienated from the psychoanalytic community and unsure of where he was heading.

After several years in a metaphorical wilderness, Jung emerged with a theory of temperament which has become a mainstay of psychology: the idea that some people are more introverted or extraverted; moreover, some use more rational (judging) or irrational (intuiting) functions of the mind. This theory carries on from Jung's emphasis on the recognition and development of opposites within the psyche: we are predisposed through genetic traits and upbringing to habitually rely on one way of meeting the world, but at some stage we need to give voice to the other in respect of what it has to offer. This, in essence, is the job of alchemy.

Unlike Freud, Jung didn't experience either parent as a domineering force in childhood, but his parents' relationship wasn't a happy one: his father, Paul, was often irritable, and his mother, Emilie, was absent for lengthy periods receiving treatment for depression. Jung's parents were chalk and cheese in terms of temperament: his father was prone to angry outbursts, his mother to the inner retreat of melancholy. And where Paul, though a pastor, wouldn't contemplate the mysteries of his religion, Emilie was interested in spiritualism and held séances at night (unknown to Paul) in the presbytery of the Jung home. For the young Carl, there was no tangled web of relationships to navigate, no extensive sibling rivalry, no confusing liaisons. Things in the Jung household were pretty straight-forward in that regard. There was just mother and father and a constant air of marital trouble in the home.

Thus, a 'problem of opposites' was front and centre during Jung's childhood. It is little wonder that the question of how to reconcile (embody) opposites on a backdrop of spiritual transcendence became Jung's life work.

Jung found answers to his quest in the work of alchemists and in Eastern philosophy: the male-female God-image of several cultures represented the Yin and Yang aspect of wholeness, relating them to the mystical experience of inner union with the divine, and thus to spiritual development. According to Jung, the mid-life crisis is a call to give expression to this spiritual aspect of the self, and thus to the wholeness of the personality.

Ironically, we can use Jung's theory on the reconciliation of opposites to explain Freud's attachment to Romain Rolland — the attachment of a man of critical reason to a modern mystic. In a letter to Rolland, as he approaches another medical procedure for jaw cancer, Freud himself gets 'all Jungian':

> Approaching life's inevitable end, reminded of it by yet another operation and aware that I am unlikely to see you again, I may confess to you that I have rarely experienced that mysterious attraction of one human being for another as vividly as I have with you; it is somehow bound up, perhaps, with the awareness of our being so different.

Perhaps if Freud had been open to Eastern concepts around balance, he might have reviewed his Oedipal theory and its one-sided notion of maturity (renunciation over fulfilment, intellectuality over sensuality, reason over intuition), and in the process address the personal nature of his childhood 'libidinous' feelings towards Amalia. This, however, would have been a huge challenge and reversal. Freud at seventy and with a legacy of work to protect, had ample reason to hold on tight.

—

From the perspective of *A Course in Miracles* we can also view Freud's resistance to the idea of transcendence, and all things 'feminine', as stemming from a fear of his own spiritual nature: the stronger the pull of the spiritual, the greater the need to defend against it. But, as the heroic myths of the ages point out, the greatest treasure is guarded by the biggest dragon. In the process of connecting with our spiritual Self, we need to look at our grievances, and this can feel daunting. Indeed, without help from our Inner Teacher who promises to lead us beyond 'the circle of fear', the task can appear to be too great.

Through the Looking Glass: Forgiveness, Time and the Event Horizon

'A picture is worth a thousand words' and our dreams are full of them. Metaphors use symbolic imagery to equate one thing with another. Familiar images are used in ways that transcend their usual meaning. For example, 'She was shadowboxing', turns the well-known term 'shadowboxing' into a symbol of someone's inner battle projected outwards onto others.

The strength of metaphors lies in their ability to hit at the heart of things. Words conveying symbolic imagery strike us in ways that literal, non-symbolic exposition can't. With imagery, we comprehend the total picture before we have a chance to dissect it with our rational mind. As such, metaphors are handy when we want to stress the importance of something.

Metaphors, Thresholds and A Course in Miracles

A Course in Miracles frequently uses metaphors and poetic language for emphasis, particularly in describing times when we're at a major crossroads in our learning. Indeed, 'crossroads' is a symbol itself, reflecting a point at which an important decision is to be made regarding our future direction. In 'The Borderland', the Course depicts such a scenario:

> There is a borderland of thought that stands between this world and Heaven. It is not a place, and when you reach it is apart from

> time. Here... all illusions are laid down beside the truth, where they are judged to be untrue. This borderland is just beyond the gate of Heaven. Here is every thought made pure and wholly simple. Here is sin denied, and everything that is received instead.[32]

Though the borderland isn't a place, we are given the metaphor of a section of land that stands before a gate of Heaven. The picture is clear and evocative: we have reached a part along a journey where we are faced with a threshold of change — will we elect to pass through the gate?

The Borderland is where we accept the Atonement Principle: that we haven't offended God, that nothing terrible has happened; we have been 'at home in God, dreaming of exile'. We recognise the illusory nature of the world of separation and separate interests, of shifting alliances and broken selves. Earlier, in Chapter 22 of the Text, the Course talks about another important threshold:

> This is a crucial period in this course, for here the separation of you and the ego must be made complete... Now must you choose between yourself and an illusion of yourself. Not both, but one.[33]

A few paragraphs later, this crucial period is described as a 'Branching of the road':

> When you come to the place where the branch in the road is quite apparent, you cannot go ahead. You must go either one way or the other. For now if you go straight ahead, the way you went before you reached the branch, you will go nowhere. The whole purpose of coming this far was to decide which branch you will take now. The way you came no longer matters. It can no longer serve.[34]

At this point in our journey, we've come too far to turn back because we know the futility of where we were headed before, but we're afraid to accept the commitment we've made to follow the Course's message. Better, says the Course, that we acknowledge that we can't turn back — that, 'A choice made with the power of Heaven to uphold it cannot be undone' — and in this acknowledgement, we are assured we will receive all that we need to keep on going. We simply need to keep the faith.

This chapter carries on with the Course's tradition of using metaphors to express the Big Stuff — those places along our way that present us with the greatest opportunity for growth, along with showing us our greatest resistance. I'd like to put forward a metaphor to help convey the radical implications of our decision to accept the Course's Atonement. I will use the Event Horizon of black holes as a symbol for a branching of the road, or a borderland. But first, a very short introduction to some strange, cosmic phenomena.

How to Make a Black Hole

The more particles you pack into a single container, the more the content density increases. If you pack enough particles of something, anything, into a constant volume of space, you will eventually make a black hole. It's as simple, and amazing, as that.

Gravity is a force that acts on an object, directing energy towards its centre. At the same time, there is outward pressure within the object's mass that matches the force of gravity, up to a point. As the density of an object increases, so too does the gravitational force acting upon it, and at some critical point the outward pressure can no longer match the gravitational force: the object collapses in on itself and seems to disappear. What remains is a hole that is the blackest of blacks and that has an extremely strong gravitational pull.

Black holes occur naturally when the core of a massive star implodes due to extreme gravitational pressure. Anything crossing the edge of the hole is swallowed forever, even light, but it has to get close enough to be pulled right in. The Event Horizon is the point where the gravitational pull of the black hole gets you, and off you go, into the great unknown: it's the horizon at which the 'event' happens.

Granted, dropping into a black hole can seem a scary prospect — heading into the unknown, perhaps (as some scientists have claimed) into another universe. Einstein's theory of gravity seems to also predict that time itself comes to an abrupt end at the centre of the hole, which is why a black hole is sometimes described as the 'reverse of creation'.

Forgiveness and the End of Time

There are a few things about this cosmic scenario that appeal to me as metaphor for transformative change. Firstly, the change involved in crossing from one side of the Event Horizon to the other is radical (to put it mildly).

With the branching of the road metaphor, we see the emphasis on choosing a different direction, on establishing our goal; 'planting our flag' on either the ego's path or the Holy Spirit's. The borderland at the gate of Heaven metaphor depicts the choice to step into peace, recognising that our belief in sin and separation has been misguided. The idea of crossing an Event Horizon into a different universe, leaving time and the past behind — the 'reverse of creation' — ups the ante on the mystery scale. It is also a useful metaphor for the radical change that emerges when one consistently accepts the Miracle. It represents a new life, a rebirth:

> Miracles are both beginnings and endings, and so they alter the temporal order. They are always affirmations of rebirth… They undo the past in the present, and thus release the future.[35]

Miracles put an end to our past grievances affecting our present experience, and so they are beginnings. Discussions of time figure a lot in the Course because our linear concept of time roots us in the ego's dream. Sin is the thought of having done something wrong in the past (the belief in separating from God), which means our experience in the present is one of guilt, and we will have fear of the future. Lock in one element of this trio and you experience them all. The choice to cross the Event Horizon and leave the past behind is therefore a choice to be free of guilt, but this also means no longer insisting that our attacks on others are justified: 'Everyone seen without the past thus brings you nearer to the end of time'.[36]

When seeming attacks bring out the fighter in us, or the walking wounded, we can remember that our goal is nothing less than to be reborn. This is reminiscent of the 'first time idea' in Workbook Lesson 7, which is not unlike Buddhism's Beginner's Mind: without thoughts of the past to project onto the present, our minds are open to the reality of what is before us now.

Life in the Fast Lane: Approaching the Event Horizon

Moving on from the past means letting go of our character armour, of the identifications we have clung to for so many years, but that aren't really us at all. And we know they're not us if they place us in opposition to others: identifications such as 'black sheep', or 'winner', 'overlooked' or 'favoured'. There is a method in the ego's madness: a sense of irreconcilable differences is what keeps it alive.

But although our character armour preserves our identification with the ego, it was once necessary. We adopted it in childhood to feel secure — it was the best we could do, faced with a frightening existence. We'll therefore experience significant inner turmoil along the path to letting it go.

And here we stand, at the Event Horizon. We are near the end zone, and though the particular forgiveness lessons are familiar, we are now dealing with them in a more profound way — their nature as reflections of the ontological split from God is now more salient. These issues are the ones that have brought us the greatest feelings of anxiety, depression, guilt, anger and shame. Intense feelings of abandonment and fear of punishment are central to them, along with one special person who has seemed to be the source of it all; the main reason for us adopting our character armour all those years ago.

Disorientation before reorientation, disintegration before integration; the turbulent process of inner change that comes from engaging in the process of forgiveness, forcing us to relinquish our armour, can limit our movements in the outer world. Though this inner process can 'save a thousand years' in terms of letting go of our ego, to outsiders it can seem like we have come to a standstill.

The Event Horizon provides another wonderful metaphor for this: if we were to observe an object at the edge of the Horizon, it would appear to be frozen in time; absolutely still. This is because (according to Einstein's Theory of Relativity) time is affected by the speed at which we are travelling — since the gravitational pull of the black hole increases as an object gets closer to it, the object will speed up as it approaches the Event Horizon, but, to a stationary observer away from the hole it will appear to be slowing down. So, during a turbulent inner shift, the world might see you as stuck, going nowhere, lost, not getting much done, but internally you are travelling at a cracking pace.

As we deal with the inner confusion, disorientation and fear associated with particular forgiveness issues, we'll gradually be able to return to the essence of the choice at hand: Do we want to see what we have denied, because it is the *Truth*? This is 'the last unanswered question' referred to in the Course, and follows on from three others: Do I desire a world I rule instead of one that rules me? Do I desire a world where I am powerful instead of helpless? Do I desire a world in which I have no enemies and cannot sin?

Though we might say yes to the first three questions, we still find the last one daunting because the ego has convinced us that Truth is our enemy. We believe we are refugees who have fled an unloving father; a tyrant who lorded it over us. To cross that threshold and return to Truth is to be met with the wrath of a punishing father: 'How dare you run away from home! What will people think?!'

If Truth is where retribution lies, we can stay away from it by focusing on our grievances, which keep us nice and safe on this side of Heaven's gate. The Course assures us, however, that 'God's Will for [us] is perfect happiness', and we begin to accept this as we let go of our belief in guilt by practicing forgiveness. We are also assured that the reality of our experience on the 'other side' of our grievances is worth the leap of faith:

> Can you imagine what a state of mind without illusions is? How it would feel? Try to remember when there was a time, — perhaps a minute, maybe even less — when nothing came to interrupt your peace; when you were certain you were loved and safe. Then try to picture what it would be like to have that moment be extended to the end of time and to eternity. Then let the sense of quiet that you felt be multiplied a hundred times, and then be multiplied another hundred more…
>
> And now you have a hint, not more than just the faintest intimation of the state your mind will rest in when the truth has come.[37]

As children we are fascinated by the idea of other worlds entered into by mysterious means: a looking glass, a wardrobe, a newly discovered door. As adults, instead of being fearful of what lies ahead if we let go of our past, we can tap into that sense of enchantment and wonder at the prospect of passing beyond the Horizon into a different universe; of being reborn. Unlike in our childhood stories, there are no battles on the other side, no riddles to solve, or struggles in order to return home. We'll know that we are home, that the only problem has been solved, and that we can call everyone friend.

The Script Is Written: Synchronicity and the Mind-World Connection

Perhaps one of the least discussed, yet most profound, teachings of *A Course in Miracles* is the idea that our lives represent a script that was both written and lived out long ago:

> The script is written... For we but see the journey from the point at which it ended, looking back on it, imagining we make it once again; reviewing mentally what has gone by.[38]

There is indeed, nothing new under the sun — it has all been said, and done. This follows from the Course's view of time. In the instant the 'tiny, mad idea' that we could be separate from God seemed to occur, the world, our individual lives, and the whole of time — past, present and future — unravelled at once, like a huge carpet being rolled out:

> Time seems to go in one direction, but when you reach its end it will roll up like a long carpet spread along the past behind you, and will disappear. As long as you believe the Son of God is guilty you will walk along this carpet, believing that it leads to death. And the journey will seem long and cruel and senseless, for so it is.[39]

The carpet is a metaphor for a linear path of cause-effect relationships, of incremental growth and of decay. It represents the ego's script, in which we identify as a body, time-bound, mortal, limited. Time *seems* to go in one direction, towards our inevitable end as a body, and this is our experience when we follow the ego's script. But with the Miracle, though time still appears to be going forward, we are really going backward in terms of undoing the carpet, returning to an awareness of our Origin.

Being the outcome of a thought of separation — of having abandoned God and destroyed his Oneness, then placing the responsibility onto God, believing that *He* abandoned *us* — the ego's life script follows along the same lines: stories of abandonment, and retribution; of feeling shamefully inferior (not good enough), and somehow harmful to others (not good).

Though the idea of scripts, already written, might seem to suggest a deterministic view of life in which free will is a myth, this is far from the truth: every possible version of our lives according to every possible decision we could ever make — a yes here, a no there, a left or a right — was included in that great carpet of time. There are therefore numerous scripts we call 'our life' to be tapped into at any moment, according to our decision to listen to the ego or the Holy Spirit and their respective messages of separate interests or shared interests, scarcity or abundance, fear or love.

To be sure, these are mind-boggling concepts, beyond the realms of any rational, scientific understanding. They're perhaps easier to grasp if we allow them to be mysterious, magical. As the Course says of time — conjuring thoughts of a magician — it is 'a trick, a sleight of hand'.

The good news is that just as the ego generates a script out of our supposed descent from Heaven — represented by a long and arduous journey along a carpet of time — the Holy Spirit provides an answer, a corrective script. This answer conveys the Atonement Principle that says we are 'at home in God, dreaming of exile':

> A Miracle is a correction. It does not create, nor really change at all. It merely looks on devastation, and reminds the mind that what it

sees is false.[40]

The Holy Spirit's corrective script runs parallel to the ego's, and we can tap into it at any time. Indeed, it's in our moments of forgiveness, of being willing to see beyond separate interests and our projections of shame and guilt, that we tap into this alternative script, in which a decision for the ego has been corrected by a decision for the Holy Spirit. Our thoughts are then forgiving thoughts and our mind is open to receive messages from the corrective script — symbols and words we encounter in the outer world that appear to meet our current psychological process and need in a profound and uncanny way.

This, of course, is Jung's notion of synchronicity, wherein there's an 'equivalence of meaning' between our psychological state and the world: they appear to be 'in sync'. These are the moments in which we're struck by a meaningful coincidence. For example, a friend, Sophie, told me that after reading my essay 'Through the Looking Glass: Forgiveness, Time and the Event Horizon' which discusses metaphors for major thresholds of change, she was taken aback by a road sign she passed whilst walking the very next day. The following account is in her own words:

> I'd been feeling restless for some time, having dreams that seemed significant but which I couldn't decipher. I walked to a park that I had been visiting for some weeks and on my way home passed a sign that I would have walked past many times without noticing. For some reason, this day, I looked up and read the warning sign, 'Event Ahead'. I was struck by this as I had never seen such a sign before and looked ahead to see what it was referring to. I saw nothing that could indicate any danger, other than a 'T' intersection. The warning seemed a bit extreme for such a seemingly benign 'event', but I felt the sign was meant for me; as if it was talking directly to me. And since I was at the time reading Patti Smith's book, *Year of The Monkey*, where throughout she has conversations

with a hotel vacancy sign, it really seemed that this was the case.

About a week later I was walking down a parallel road, and a temporary sign displayed the same warning: 'Event Ahead'. Again, I was struck by this. Why didn't it just say 'Roadworks Ahead'? I was now sure that this was meant for me and I needed to be prepared. A few weeks later the event did occur, and, although to someone else the situation may not have seemed all that important, the fear and anxiety that it produced told me it was a significant moment for me. A decision had to be made, and I had to face this fear.

The 'event' was challenging, but also rich with possibility for change, and Sophie's mindful approach towards it as such an opportunity helped her work through it and achieve a positive sense of resolution.

Moments of synchronicity function as guidance. In those Holy Instants in which we choose forgiveness and hear the Holy Spirit, we tap into that parallel correction script, and this will be reflected in choices we make. I recently reflected on one such moment I myself experienced a few years ago. I'd been experiencing a Dark Night of the Soul for what seemed to be an eternity, and was finally feeling like I was emerging — albeit slowly — from those subterranean depths. The problem was that it had been such an intense time that a shadow of the 'wobbliness' associated with it was following me around, making me doubt my strength and readiness to emerge.

I got up one morning and decided to walk to my local op shop (Charity Store) and check out their books. I love looking at the book collections in these stores; they are so eclectic. Scouring the shelves for anything enticing, I turned a corner and saw a book curiously laid out on its own on a shelf right in front of me. I noticed it was old, in good condition, and a hardback.

Having hit upon signed first editions here before, I immediately picked up the book and opened the cover. Sure enough, it was a signed first edition of a James Bond novel. Not into Bond, but swayed by a signed first edition, I purchased the book for three dollars.

I went for a walk in a park later that day, and as I took in the familiar surrounds a thought spontaneously crossed my mind: 'The title of the book'. And then it hit me. The book was called *Licence Renewed* — the first in a second series of Bond books, taking up where Bond's career as a 00 agent had ended (after the agency disbanded), but was now being renewed as an independent 'trouble-shooter' for MI-6.

'Licence Renewed': I had received the affirmation I needed to end my self-doubt, and I had received it (having gone to the bookshop and recognised the relevance of the title) because my goal had been to keep moving forward along my path of forgiveness, and I evidently needed to know I was indeed growing in strength. I had tuned in to the Holy Spirit's correction script in those moments, and received the guidance I needed.

In any given instant, we can avail ourselves of the Holy Spirit's script. We just need to choose forgiveness as our goal and listen. But we won't be able to listen if we're full of resentment or choose to indulge our grievances. We simply need a little willingness to be steadfast in our goal of awakening, and as we move forward, we can rest in the knowledge that a greater strength goes with us:

> The Atonement is so gentle you need but whisper to it, and all its power will rush to your assistance and support. You are not frail with God beside you.[41]

Living Colour: Wholeness, Integration and Our One Self

Two messages are famously inscribed on the Temple of Apollo at Delphi, Greece: 'Nothing in excess', and 'Know thyself'. The first seems obvious: too much of this or that and you'll make yourself sick. The second, 'Know thyself', is a little more complicated: *Which* self?!

As teenagers, the question of identity looms large: Who do we want to be? Where do we want to go? What do we want to do? It takes half a lifetime to realise that life isn't all it's cracked up to be. The roles we've chosen haven't satisfied us as we thought they might, intimate relationships are more trying than the romantic ideal led us to believe, and there is no 'sure thing' in the entire universe. We begin to be haunted by the existential thought 'What's it all for?' Have we been sold a lie?

The question of life's meaning is intimately connected to our self-concept. In the second half of life, and perhaps several careers/relationships later, we need to realise the importance of the question, 'Who am I?' yet again. In his interviews with Bill Moyers (*The Power of Myth*, 1988), the mythologist Joseph Campbell said that when people say they're seeking meaning in life, what they're really wanting is an experience of being alive. I think there's a lot of truth in that. In the course of finding our way through life we neglect parts of ourselves in order to fit in. Though we might develop a strong sense of self, it is a negotiated identity — we're not fully ourselves and so life takes on a lacklustre hue: our strong sense of self has only got us so far. Perhaps we've got along as an independent type, a community-minded individual, or an ambitious self-starter. There comes a time of reckoning, however, when we need to question if our familiar list of attributes is giving us the whole picture.

Our Divided Self

You're likely familiar with the term 'repression' and the Freudian idea of pushing something anxiety-producing into your unconscious. Dissociation also stems from a need to keep anxiety at bay, but the anxiety relates to having two aspects of ourselves that, due to their opposing nature, we can't embody at the same time. We can't, for example, act out aggressively towards someone, yet show them tenderness and care in the very same moment: we can switch gears after our outburst, but we can't be two people at once.

Likewise, there are aspects of our personality that contradict each other, and rather than deal with the anxiety that comes with looking at these aspects side by side (so we can resolve the issues at the heart of their extremes and come to a more balanced place), we split them off from each other; we 'dissociate' them.

These split-off parts function like sub-personalities, complete units in their own right. Carl Jung called them complexes: groups of ideas and beliefs which have particular emotions, reactions, memories, and self-identities associated with them. If we feel rejected, for example, we might tap into a whole collection of feelings, memories, and self-beliefs that equate to one type of personality — perhaps we withdraw, feeling forlorn. On another day, rejection might elicit a very different response, way on the opposite side of the scale with different associated memories and self-beliefs — this time, we erupt in anger and storm about. And because opposite complexes can't 'live in the same house', we alternate between them. Sometimes we stay at mum's, sometimes we stay at dad's (and though these are metaphors, it's a good opportunity to point out that many of our complexes develop in response to our parents — either from attachment to a parent, a reaction against one, or from both these motives).

While Freud talked a lot about repression as a psychological defence to anxiety, Jung's analytical psychology focuses on dissociation. Freud was interested in what the dominant personality — the 'I' — repressed in relation to its own, linear experience of life (including traumatic events). Jung was interested in the parallel lives we lead; in how we deal with the opposites within us. He realised that many characteristics we consciously own have a dissociated opposite in our unconscious. Indeed, our conscious aspect was most likely adopted as a defence against its dissociated partner.

A famous case of dissociation in popular culture is that of Dr Jekyll and Mr Hyde. The good doctor is a kind man, professional and refined. His alter-ego is violent and malevolent. Jung calls this dark aspect of our personality the shadow, and the family-friendly face the persona. The latter is something akin to a public relations exercise, but if we identify with it too much — try too hard to deny our irritations and the like — our shadow side will eventually make a liar out of us, slipping out when we least expect it, compulsively and perhaps dangerously.

Some people let their alter-ego breathe in a formalised way. They find an outlet for it in groups tailored to special interests and fetishes; the dark, hidden venues of the past now somewhat superseded by online environments. But outside of these arenas, a very different life is led under the guise of the persona, and this is possible via to the process of dissociation: the person at the club isn't the same person at the pulpit.

Our personality is fragmented into sub-personalities that can exist side by side because they never meet: the right hand doesn't know what the left hand is doing; at least, that's the case while we're identified with either extreme. With insight we can reflect on how we're one person this day, another the next, but when we're actually occupying either of those opposites, the reactions, thoughts, self-concept and memories of the other side are dissociated from consciousness.

It's Not Me, It's You

We can become aware of our shadow by noticing our reactions to other people. If there are traits we can't stand in someone else, this means we have judged ourselves harshly for the very same traits (albeit, they might be expressed in a different way), and so we have decided to disown, or dissociate, them because they cause us anxiety. Says Jung in *Archaic Man*:

> Everything that is unconscious in ourselves we discover in our neighbour, and we treat him accordingly... we injure him by means of moral verdicts pronounced with the deepest conviction. What we combat in him is usually our inferior [dissociated] side.

For example, if I find someone to be repugnantly selfish, I must have at some stage noticed a degree of selfishness in myself and condemned myself for it. I'm likely to then overcompensate for my 'sinful' nature by neglecting my own self-care and spreading myself thin by putting the needs of others first.

Jung saw ultimate meaning in embodying the totality of our personality — our search for wholeness and to feel alive is the search for an undivided self. Thus, Jung called the process of integration 'individuation'. Not only can we be repelled by aspects of ourselves projected onto others, we can be attracted by aspects we've dissociated as well. This is the case in infatuation: we are spellbound by the positive aspect of something we have dissociated within ourselves and therefore feel we lack. If we are fearful of our destructive power, for example, we'll be attracted to people who appear powerful in helpful, constructive ways.

This relates to the 'search for completion' discussed in the Course. What we seek for in another is our undivided, whole self — a sense of completion that can only come from within. In relation to *A Course in Miracles*, Freud's emphasis on repression comes to the fore regarding the repressed, traumatic thought that we have separated from God, destroyed His Oneness and now await his certain reprimand. Jung's emphasis on dissociation relates to the Course's discussion of our search for completion and wholeness; in ending our dissociations within, and without, through the process of forgiveness.

There is no concept of reconciliation with Freud — the idea of two things coming together (within our minds) to sort out their differences and look at each other anew. Freud gives us the psychoanalytic equivalent of our authority problem with God via his theory of the Oedipus Complex. Meanwhile, Jung gives us the psychoanalytic equivalent of the Course's forgiveness through his 'reconciliation of opposites'; an inner split reflected in the way we relate to others. As he says in 'Psychology and Religion: West and East':

> Neurosis is an inner cleavage — the state of being at war with oneself. Everything that accentuates this cleavage makes the patient worse, and everything that mitigates it tends to heal him. What drives people to war with themselves is the suspicion or the knowledge that they consist of two persons in opposition to one another... A neurosis is a splitting of personality.

One aspect of the personality is likely to be dominant, more habitual, than the other, but which one really represents 'us'? In his wonderful, paradoxical way, Jung would answer 'Both, but neither': in order to end the dissociation of these complexes within us, we have to first acknowledge that both are there. Neither one on their own represents who we really are, but when brought together — that is, acknowledged within our mind, where their differences can be 'reconciled' — something different to their extremes is brought forth. Then we have what Jung called the 'irrational third'.

Healing and the Irrational Third

The 'third' is irrational because we don't come to it by rational means. In other words, it's not arrived at through a contrived process of trying to balance our opposing tendencies, like we're baking a cake (or creating Milton the Monster: 'Six drops of the essence of terror, five drops of sinister sauce... And now for a touch of tenderness.... Oops, too much!'). Instead, it comes through a process that is very much like the Course's description of forgiveness.

The first step in the Course's forgiveness process is to acknowledge that we're never upset by a fact but by our interpretation of it. This is important and empowering because it refocuses our attention within rather than without. We then accept that what we are judging harshly in someone else, we have already condemned in ourselves. Indeed, it's because we have judged ourselves harshly that we feel a need to sentence someone else.

'Would I condemn myself for this?' is a question the Course suggests we ask whenever we feel angered by the actions of others. We might not have done the exact same thing in form, but have had the same attitude at some stage. By then asking the Holy Spirit for help to look on our self-accusation from the perspective of Truth (which affirms the innocence of our true Self) we are able to let go of our guilt.

In the Jungian tradition, we acknowledge what we see in another is also within ourselves, and that we have adopted the opposite conscious attitude as compensation. We make conscious the attitudes — the complex — we have dissociated and address why we might have dissociated it in the first place. What felt dangerous about it? Did the idea of a capacity for tenderness and kindness make us feel vulnerable? Did the prospect of self-assertion make us fear punishment and calamity?

Jung's analytical psychology is also forward-looking — why has the issue come up *now*? If we we're to embrace the positive aspects of what we dissociated, what would we be able to do going forward? We then develop a 'religious attitude'; opening our minds to help from something that transcends the ego 'I'. Jung sometimes called this something the Holy Ghost, reflecting its Biblical function as a source of inspiration and support in fulfilling God's Will. Just as the Apostles huddled together, fearful and grieving after the crucifixion, were visited by the Holy Spirit who ended their inner conflict and inspired strength, so too, says Jung in 'A Psychological Approach to the Trinity', does something transcendent within our psyche end the conflict involved in reconciling opposites, leaving us renewed:

> This spirit is an autonomous psychic happening, a hush that follows the storm, a reconciling light in the darkness of man's mind, secretly bringing order into the chaos of his soul.

The tension between opposites is difficult to bring into awareness because conflict comes with it, both within and without. What we battle to encompass within ourselves will reflect in our treatment of someone else. The temptation will be to push that someone away — to keep a gap between you, effectively exiling this dissociated part of yourself. And if one person moves more to their extreme to keep away, the other — repelled by the dissociated aspect they see outside them — may move further into their extreme.

Spirit and Matter: Clash of the Titans

Of all the opposites to preoccupy the musings of philosophers and religious folk throughout the ages, spirit and matter have to rank highest. In one corner, we have the seen, the tangible, the world apprehended by our body's five senses. In the opposite corner, we have something invisible, mysterious, unknowable yet familiar to us on some inexpressible level. How on earth do these two things meet, if indeed they meet at all? And most importantly, who will win?

Here, as everywhere, we first need to clarify our terms in order to escape confusion. Readers of the Course will be familiar with its unique definition of traditional Christian terms such as forgiveness and atonement. Jung's analytical psychology also has its definitions for traditional spiritual terms. Where the Course talks about spirit and our Self as being part of a Oneness outside time and space, Jung keeps his definitions rooted in psychological experience and outside the realm of religious faith.

While the Jungian use of spirit (and the symbol of the Holy Ghost) relates to a higher consciousness, to a power beyond our own resources, a source of insight and good advice — unseen, unchanging and impersonal — Jung stops there. In other words, he describes spirit as something that makes contact with our personal psyche in this world, but doesn't talk of it existing outside time and space, as the Course would describe it.

Jung never strayed from his 'job description' as a psychologist, and so his concepts of the Self and spirit don't extend into the realm of traditional spiritual metaphysics. Jung was all about what we experience, rather than ultimate truths. Jung's use of the terms spirit and Self don't relate to the spiritual metaphysics of the Course, but they *do* relate to our experience of a guiding force, leading to an appreciation of our wholeness: something akin to the Holy Spirit's voice and the memory of our one Self in what the Course calls our 'right mind'.

When Jung speaks of reconciliation between 'spirit and matter', therefore, he isn't talking about trying to reconcile the irreconcilable (Truth with illusion), but of achieving a dialogue between that part of us that seeks inner fulfilment and growth, with how we live our daily lives. He's talking about yoga in its most fundamental sense: how we 'yoke' our activity in the world to the aims and inspiration of that which transcends the ego 'I'. This brings us back to Joseph Campbell's sentiment mentioned at the beginning of this discussion. If in seeking meaning we are really seeking for an experience of being alive, then 'Yoga' is the way of achieving it. As Campbell said in his interview with Bill Moyers (*The Power of Myth*, 1988):

> I think what we're looking for is a way of experiencing the world in which we are living that will open to us the transcendence that

informs it, and at the same time informs ourselves within it. That's what people want, that's what the soul asks for.

The conflict between our material and spiritual selves is often personified along stereotypical lines — we've imagined caricatures of what it is to be spiritual, or material. We've associated spirituality with self-denial, going out of our way for other people, compliance and overall saintliness. On the other side of the spectrum, we have 'sensual man': a narcissistic, domineering species, often found in the upper echelons of business. The choice before us is stark, each option leading to vastly different worlds. Neither the saint nor the opportunist understands the other; one appears as weak and vulnerable, the other as selfish and superficial.

Reflecting back on those wise words at the Temple of Apollo, both of the above 'solutions to life' embody an excess. And because of the things we traditionally associate with 'masculine' and 'feminine', we are often swayed one way or the other according to gender expectations — which also means that neurotic extremes have historically been socially endorsed.

Salvation and Our One Self

To know when we're not identifying with the memory of our one Self but with extremes instead, we can follow the Course's Workbook Lesson 35, noticing when we feel imposed upon, victorious, helpless, charitable, or losing out, and then remind ourselves of the truth of our holiness. This statement of truth reminds us that when we have identified with an extreme — with one side of an equation — we have judged against our holiness, as well as our wholeness.

From a Jungian perspective, all these judgements have emotions and memories attached to them, representing a 'fragmented' personality, or a complex. When we feel victorious, we embody the associated complex, and likewise when we feel helpless, or charitable. And from a Course perspective, these personalities will each take on a hue of either victimiser or victim, winner or loser. It's a pretty dull dichotomy, but that's the range on our palette when we're painting a picture of 'one or the other'.

The Course's workbook lessons are designed to end the dissociation between what we believe about ourselves and the reality of who we are. Their statements of truth aren't positive affirmations to shout down our mistaken beliefs. Rather, they are means of illuminating darkness. In many places the Course says that we can't reconcile the irreconcilable — that truth and error can't meet because only one really exists (see for example T-10.IV.2:5). This is true on a mechanistic level: two things can't meet if only one exists. On the level of *belief*, however, we need to look at things together, side by side, in order to see what we are choosing between and the consequences of our choice.

In summary, by enduring the conflict, confusion, and fatigue that comes with ending our inner and outer dissociations — reconciling opposites — something new, more vibrant, emerges: a monochrome life becomes one of living colour. Instead of a battle between polarities, we now embody the best of both worlds, which really means the wholeness of our Self, both in terms of our personality and our spiritual being.

Klein and A Course in Miracles: On Love, Loss and the Centrality of the Atonement Principle

In previous chapters I've drawn distinctions between the theories of Freud and Jung and how they relate to *A Course in Miracles*. The childhoods of both pioneers can clearly be seen to have influenced their theories, and their differences. In Part Two of *The Split: Freud, Jung and the Oceanic Feeling*, I show how Freud's Oedipus theory (that we want the exclusive love of a parent and have death wishes towards the other, whom we perceive as a love-rival) developed out of his relationship with his mother — an emotionally domineering figure. Similarly, I discuss how Jung's otherworldly childhood encounters led to his openness towards experiences that can't be explained by scientific rationalism.

Melanie Klein is another pioneer in psychology whose theories have grown out of her childhood experiences. The capstone to her lifetime's work was her theory of the Depressive Position, which relates to an overwhelming feeling of loss. This chapter explores her thoughts on the Depressive Position, using them to elucidate principles from the Course.

When we are depressed, it is useful to realise that we have identified as a separated self. However, to be able to take our experience of depression and trace it to something more immediate to us — something closer in time and space — gives us a greater sense of agency in dealing with our depression. We now know how our experience of loss on a metaphysical level is being represented symbolically in the here and now, and that in itself can bring significant relief.

Indeed, in Klein's psychoanalytic work with young children — in which the child was free to play with toys while Klein observed their play for clues to inner conflicts — Klein found that if she interpreted the child's play to them, the effect on the child was often striking: anxiety might increase momentarily, but then was followed by obvious relief and freer play and speech. Says Klein in *The Psychoanalytic Play Technique*:

> It was always part of my technique not to use educative or moral influence, but to keep to the psychoanalytic procedure only, which, to put it in a nutshell, consists in understanding the patient's mind and conveying to him what goes on in it.

Likewise, Carl Jung in *Psychology and Alchemy* describes how conscious insight into what is going on for us can help relieve a sense of inner turmoil that otherwise has no grounding:

> It is absolutely necessary to supply these fantastic images [in dreams, for example] that rise up so strange and threatening before the mind's eye with a sort of context so as to make them more intelligible... for the purpose of calming and clarifying a consciousness that is all at sea.

So, with such an aim in mind, let me introduce the inspiring work of Melanie Klein, beginning with a brief summary of her early life.

Setting the Stage: Klein's Early Years

Melanie Klein was born in Vienna in 1887, the youngest of four children to Moriz and Libussa Reizes. Moriz was a doctor, dentist, and a Jewish scholar, and Libussa was the granddaughter of a rabbi. Despite living at a time when the roles of men and women were strictly prescribed, intellectual pursuits in the Reizes household weren't restricted along gender lines. Melanie wished to become a doctor, and her parents obliged by sending her to university. In contrast, Freud didn't allow his daughter Anna — or indeed, any of his daughters — to go to university, as he believed their destiny lay in marriage. Anna (who never married) went to teaching school instead, and later became a critic of Melanie Klein's work.

Melanie's first major experience of loss occurred when she was four and her older sister, whom she idolised, died. Later, at age eighteen and while she was studying medicine at university, Melanie's father died. The family was left with meagre financial reserves, and so Melanie had to let go of her dream of becoming a doctor. She withdrew from her course, undoubtedly experienced as yet another loss, and two years later one of her brothers died.

One year after her brother's death, and having left the pathway to a career, Melanie married Arthur Klein, an engineer. The marriage wasn't a happy one, and following the birth of her two children Melanie suffered from severe depression on several occasions. During these times, her mother helped look after the household while Melanie went away for treatment. In her autobiography, Melanie describes how her depression was accompanied by guilt for not being the mother to her children she wanted to be — an experience familiar to many parents, their depression compounded by the thought that their illness is hurting their loved ones.

Things improved for Melanie in 1910 when Arthur found a job in Budapest and the family moved there. Melanie received help for a nervous complaint and she came across Sigmund Freud's *The Interpretation of Dreams*. So began her interest in psychoanalysis, an interest that was a source of healing in itself: having had to leave her study of medicine behind, Melanie was now able to indulge her interest in the medical field, albeit through psychology.

Four years after the move to Budapest, Melanie gave birth to her third child, Erich, and a few months later her mother died. Distraught and seeking help, she started having psychoanalytic therapy. This strengthened her interest in psychoanalysis, and at forty-one she enrolled in a course of psychoanalytic training at an institute in Berlin, where she also had further analysis with Karl Abraham, a leading figure in the psychoanalytic community. After a year under the guiding and paternal influence of Abraham, Melanie yet again had to say her goodbyes. Abraham died unexpectedly from a lung infection at the age of forty-eight. Ten years later, Melanie's son Hans would die in a climbing accident, catalysing the bringing together of her ideas on bereavement and depression.

The general theme of loss returned to Melanie when — now living in London — her eldest child and only daughter Melitta, who was also a psychoanalyst, publicly took Anna Freud's side in a controversial split between those who agreed with Anna's theories on child therapy, and those who agreed with Melanie. Not only did Melitta disagree with her mother, but she cut ties with her, immigrating to the United States. Melitta returned to live in London after Melanie's death in 1960.

Love, Loss and the Depressive Position

In relation to the Course, Sigmund Freud gives us the psychology of 'the authority problem' — of a perceived battle between ourselves and an authority figure in order to have our need for exclusive love and attention, for specialness, filled. Freud gives us the fear of the castigating Father — the punitive God — and emphasises the influence of anxiety in our development. From Melanie Klein we can add a theory of depression which reflects the 'tiny, mad idea' in the Course's creation myth: that we can hurt that which we love; that we can lose that which we love. Says the Course:

> Children are born into [this world] through pain and in pain. Their growth is attended by suffering, and they learn of sorrow and

separation and death... They seem to love, yet they desert and are deserted. They appear to lose what they love, perhaps the most insane belief of all.[42]

Of course, believing that we've lost something dear to us doesn't seem like a 'tiny, mad idea' at all. Loss in this world is universal — we lose people and things that we love all the time. (The American author Elizabeth Bishop wrote about this beautifully in her poem *One Art*.) What the Course describes here is the idea that we are all connected on a fundamental level that is beyond the body, and the essence of that level is love. Yet, until we live with that awareness, we will have the kind of experience Klein describes.

Klein developed a model for what goes on psychologically for very young children and infants. With Freud, we have a father-centred theory, focusing on a fear of retribution. With Klein we have a mother-centred theory in which the infant's experience of being fed is paramount. Today, we know that feeding and punishment aren't allocated as strictly according to the roles of father and mother. It's not the gender that's the issue, it's the function that a person serves in relation to the child.

The depressive position comes about through ambivalent feelings towards those who feed us. To understand the intensity of the infant's feelings of love and hate, we need to understand their acute anxiety. The infant at birth is in a precarious situation: there's the trauma of birth, then an experience of enormous frustration due to the fact that it's not being nurtured in the way it was in the womb where its needs were automatically met. Now outside the womb, the infant doesn't have any sense of continuity. This is its first experience of deprivation, and it doesn't know what comes next. Will it be fed? Will the pain cease?

If you have a sense of continuity when you're undergoing frustration, you can remember how you were eventually satisfied before, and this helps you get through the frustration. For a newborn, however, the sense of frustration is total, and for the first few months of life — until a sense of continuity is established between frustration and fulfilment — the infant is exposed to very high levels of anxiety, and so begins the experience of hate; of attacking what it thinks has deprived it.

While the infant hates the parent for not feeding them on demand, it also has love for them because of the times they were attended to. The infant's experience is therefore characterised by ambivalence, by both love and hate. So, while attacks on a loved one can lead to a fear of retribution, they can also elicit great sadness at the thought of having hurt someone we love, perhaps even destroyed and lost them.

The theme of loss is at the heart of the Depressive Position, and is also addressed in sections of the Course that describe our feelings of alienation, using metaphors such as 'the forgotten song':

> Listen,— perhaps you catch a hint of an ancient state not quite forgotten; dim, perhaps, and yet not altogether unfamiliar, like a song whose name is long forgotten, and the circumstances in which you heard completely unremembered. Not the whole song has stayed with you, but just a little wisp of melody, attached not to a person or a place or anything particular. But you remember, from just this little part, how lovely was the song, how wonderful the setting where you heard it, and how you loved those who were there and listened with you.[43]

The depression that comes from our attack on those whom we love is compounded by (indeed, has its *source* in) this ancient memory of loss. It is devastating, disheartening and fatiguing, yet we have no idea why we feel the way we do. Perhaps we understand the metaphysics behind our pain, perhaps we understand it from a Kleinian point of view, but separately, these notions are of little consolation. Taken together, however, the understanding we get on both the metaphysical and worldly levels can help a great deal: we know what our pain is related to in the here and now of our human experience, and we know that we can call on help from our Inner Teacher to deal with it.

While Klein's Depressive Position helps explain our rapid dive after attacking (mentally or behaviourally) a loved one, experience will tell us that we don't always feel this way afterwards: sometimes we can go off on our merry way, perhaps even feeling triumphant rather than forlorn. Klein has another explanation for this, found in her theory of splitting and the Paranoid Schizoid Position.

Splitting and the Paranoid Schizoid Position

The Depressive Position involves recognition that we both love and hate the same person. In Klein's theory, an infant first experiences this in the second half of their first year. Before then, the infant doesn't relate to people as whole persons, but instead relates to objects — the breast, the bottle. As we've seen, the infant is dominated by intense feelings of love and hate, and they project these feelings onto objects — the 'good breast', which responds to their hunger, and the 'bad breast', which doesn't. In the infant's mind, the good breast is split from the bad — hence the 'schizoid' aspect of the position. And while the good becomes idealised, the bad is seen as a hated persecutor — hence the 'paranoid' aspect.

Later on, we develop the capacity to see the whole person behind the split objects: to see that what feeds us on demand, and what doesn't, are actually one and the same person. This is a milestone in development, but it brings with it a new source of anxiety — the thought that we can hurt or lose someone we love due to our own attack. To defend against this anxiety, we can split the loved and hated object back into two, thereby avoiding depressive despair — we either hate them, or love them, but won't allow contradictory feelings into our awareness. Further to this, when we're in the 'hate' zone we will only perceive things in a way that justifies and reinforces our position.

An experience I had recently illustrates this kind of situation. I was visiting a friend at her home, and another friend of hers came over with her adult son. The conversation was very pleasant except for the occasional surly comment made by the son in reply to his mother. He wasn't cruel, but seemed perpetually annoyed by her comments. Yet here he was, agreeing to visit a friend with her. Klein's theory makes sense of this scenario: the son loved his mother but also had unresolved anger, and to protect himself from the depressive despair associated with hurting her, he split off his love, leaving his anger in the form of annoyance.

This leads in to another way in which we can deal with the fear of loss: we can employ what Klein called 'manic defences'. Since depressive despair occurs over the loss of a valued person, manic defences are designed to deny his or her value. We can become controlling to deny our dependence on them, or contemptuous, in order to depreciate their worth.

The splitting defence helps explain something that has always perplexed me about the composer Ludwig van Beethoven. While he could compose beautiful music, he could also be horrible to people in his daily life, and on a regular basis! While Beethoven did suffer from depression periodically (especially related to the decline of his hearing), his is generally regarded as having a confrontational, narcissistic personality. Beethoven characterised many aspects of the Paranoid Schizoid Position. He saw people as either all good or all bad (his mother an angel, his father a devil); had paranoid suspicions that people were out to get him — to swindle him, accuse him of things unfairly, or even to poison him; and, he also seems to have had hypochondria which, according to Klein, is characteristic of the Paranoid Schizoid Position — persecutory fears experienced as an internal threat.

According to Klein, we need to trust that our love is greater than our hate in order to tolerate ambivalent feelings towards something. If we can't do that, we don't yet trust in our own goodness. In Klein's theory, the way we develop faith in our goodness is by having more good experiences than bad, and by engaging in attempts at reparation when we feel we've hurt someone, our kindness giving us faith in our own goodness. Our own hatred also becomes less frightening as we see that nothing disastrous happens if we express our anger — the loved one doesn't die as we might have imagined, for example.

All of this is particularly relevant for children; no one would argue the important influence of environmental factors on a child's self-concept. As adults, however, rather than relying on the world to establish a belief in our goodness, we are better off seeking to undo the self-concept we have learned. After all, our sense of loss and our persecutory fears have their root in believing we've hurt God and that He couldn't possibly love us. And so, no one and nothing outside of us can make up for that. Recognising this is the first step towards healing.

No Harm Done: the Atonement Principle

'And who could weep but for his innocence?', says the Course. Our greatest desire is to know that we haven't destroyed God's Love. The Course assures us that 'not one note in Heaven's song' has been missed, nor can we truly hurt others because we can't take the peace of God away from them. We just don't have that power. The Atonement Principle says that the separation from God — the destruction of His Love and Oneness — never occurred, because God's Love can't be destroyed:

> Joining the Atonement is the way out of fear... Truth is beyond your ability to destroy... Nothing that is good can be lost because it comes from the Holy Spirit, the Voice for creation...[44]

> What God creates is safe from all corruption, unchanged and perfect in eternity.[45]

The Atonement Principle is the Course's 'good news', however we resist its message because to say Love can't be destroyed is also to say that the ego and our special, separated self are, quite frankly, nothing. But we want to be something! The same demand for specialness that seemed to cause the dream of separation in the first place keeps us choosing our guilty and shameful self-concept, and the perception of loss.

When we feel depressed for seemingly no good reason, we can review our minds for judgements and attack. The perspective of Truth says that nothing we do, or anyone else does, has the power to affect the peace of God within our minds, because Love can't be destroyed. The following passage from the Course is a beautiful reminder that all that is true, all that exists, all that lasts, are the loving thoughts we share:

> All your past except its beauty is gone, and nothing is left but a blessing. I have saved all your kindnesses and every loving thought you ever had. I have purified them of the errors that hid their light, and kept them for you in their own perfect radiance. They are beyond destruction and beyond guilt. They came from the Holy Spirit within you, and we know what God creates is eternal... The Thoughts of God are with you.[46]

All of us have things we are sorry for in our past. We regret our actions, and perhaps have tried to make amends or otherwise been held accountable. This is normal and helpful: remorse can motivate us to be kinder, change our ways, or otherwise not intentionally attack others in the future. But getting stuck in guilt is excruciating and can adversely affect all our relationships because we become so self-absorbed in it. I'm reminded of the music video 'Hurt' by Johnny Cash. It is such a poignant song and clip about being stuck in guilt. As June Carter castes a deeply concerned gaze at her tortured husband, we see she too suffers as he seems lost to her in his pain. No one wins when you're stuck in guilt.

Just as we need help to forgive others, we need help to forgive ourselves: the Holy Spirit reminds us of our other Self, our true Self, and it is this reminder that is the ultimate healing agent. This might motivate us to do certain things to redress our guilt, or lead us to something that helps us forgive someone by gaining an understanding of their situation or state of mind, but healing begins with our willingness to join with that memory of our one Self. Without this help — some connection with this memory — true forgiveness, which is based on the principle of our unassailable wholeness, is impossible.

Seeing the Problem as It Is—Part I: Karen Horney's Defensive Solutions

Half the battle in applying the principles of *A Course in Miracles* is being aware of when we've chosen to the listen to the ego. The Course tells us that we know we're not listening to the Holy Spirit if peace isn't in our awareness. But we also know through experience that a detour away from peace can begin very subtly, as the Course warns:

> ... take not one step in the descent to hell. For having taken one, you will not recognize the rest for what they are. And they will follow.[47]

Sometimes our choosing of the ego feels good, other times it feels bad. As Workbook Lesson 20 states, we can't tell the difference between pleasure and pain:

> You want salvation. You want to be happy. You want peace. You do not have them now, because your mind is totally undisciplined, and you cannot distinguish between joy and sorrow, pleasure and pain, love and fear.

Learning how to tell pleasure and pain apart is what the Course's curriculum is for. The pleasure of conquest, for example, isn't the positive thing it appears to be. To value conquest is to 'value the valueless', leading to depression and despair because we've valued something that can't be shared. In this schema we are a 'winner', someone else a 'loser' and this means we've cut our awareness off from the abundance and wholeness of our true Self. If we have chosen to identify with the ego, therefore, we might feel good but on some level we'll experience anxiety from dissociating an awareness of Source.

The Course describes how psychological projection is a defence to such anxiety, which stems from guilt over our choice to turn our back on God. Feeling guilty, we try and decrease our fear of God's punishment by projecting the guilt outwards and onto other people. If we feel angry towards someone else, then that's a sure sign that we have chosen to identify with the ego. Indeed, the whole world — according to the Course's metaphysical underpinnings — serves as one big defence for our guilt over separating from God. It's a place in which we seem to be victimised by everyone and everything on a daily basis, and have ample cause to perceive the evil-doer 'out there'.

Familiarising ourselves with defences to anxiety is therefore an important way of knowing when we've chosen to identify with the ego. Projection isn't the only defence: there are plenty more.

The Defence Department

Sigmund Freud was the first in his scientific field to recognise the importance of anxiety in understanding psychological disorders generally. Freud had been investigating hysterical neurosis, which was the term for someone suffering from physical symptoms without any discernible physical cause. Under hypnosis, the ailment mysteriously disappeared. A person who'd lost their voice could talk; someone who couldn't raise their arm could now move it effortlessly.

Hysterical neurosis was most commonly diagnosed in women, and as its name suggests, was at one stage thought to be caused by a wandering womb (the word 'hysterical' being derived from the Latin *hystericus* meaning 'of the womb'). Of course, this meant that men couldn't be diagnosed with hysteria, and so, quite simply, they weren't (men who displayed the symptomology of hysterical neurosis were simply given a different diagnosis). Freud, however, went against the grain by suggesting that a repressed traumatic experience — rather than anything to do with a womb — was the cause of hysterical neurosis. The repressed memory, or conflict, was a source of anxiety, and the physical symptoms were the result.

For Freud, anxiety comes about through 'dynamic inner conflict', from having to repress something central to your being, something instinctual. The two main instincts that we do battle with throughout our lives, according to Freud, are Eros and Thanatos: the life and death instincts. Roughly speaking, Eros relates to sexuality, reproduction of the species and love (which to Freud was a feeling linked to a biological imperative to preserve and build upon life); Thanatos to aggression, hate and violence generated by a drive to return to an inorganic (dead) state.

Eros is constructive, Thanatos is destructive, and they occur together, but Thanatos is usually the quieter of the two in our conscious mind — instead of destroying ourselves, we displace our hatred (the death instinct) outwards in the form of violence and aggression towards others. Or, being civilised creatures, we sublimate these feelings by discharging them through exercise, or creating something. Displacement and sublimation are two defences we can use to minimise feelings of anxiety that arise if either Eros or Thanatos are frustrated by our environment (society, parents, opportunity). It is useful to explore these defences a little further, along with others put forward by Freud:

Repression: When a feeling, memory or perception is forced from consciousness to the unconscious because it is seen as socially unacceptable.

Displacement: When we direct strong emotions and frustrations toward a person or object that doesn't feel threatening. For example, instead of yelling at my boss, I yell at a politician on television.

Projection: When we feel guilty about an emotion or a judgement so project that feeling onto someone else. For example, if I hate my boss but feel guilty about it, I can project my hatred onto them, perceiving them as the one who hates me.

Reaction formation: When we act the opposite way to how we feel because the original sensation causes anxiety. For example, I hate my boss but act as if I adore him or her.

Sublimation: Instead of acting on my anger, I channel it into something that vents my energy in a non-harmful way, such as playing sport.

Denial: When we simply refuse to accept reality or facts. 'I don't know what you're talking about. I'm not angry at my boss'.

Freud's concept of anxiety is rooted in the idea of instincts and what happens if the energy associated with their expression is blocked by the environment. According to Freud the energy builds up and produces tension leading to 'nervous excitation', or 'anxiety'. Pleasure is what we experience when this tension is released. In this theory, relationships are only relevant in how they mould the expression of instinctual energy — how they affect the overall 'hydraulics' of the individual's system. Freud's is a mechanistic, biological view that neglects the powerful role of relationships in *creating* aggression, for example, not merely channelling it. For another perspective, we need to look further afield to what has come to be known as the Cultural School of psychoanalysis.

Karen Horney, a leading figure in the Cultural School, provides insights into the relational origins of anxiety, and of defensive structures we adopt to deal with it. Horney's clearly articulated theory of defences offers us a great deal in terms of understanding behavioural patterns and their motivations, helping us further discern when we have chosen to identify with the ego.

Horney's Sociological Perspective

Karen Horney was a German psychoanalyst who practiced in the United States later in her career, and founded the *American Journal of Psychoanalysis*, serving as its editor until her death in 1952. She is one of the founders of feminist psychology, and rejected Freud's emphasis on biology in determining behaviour and anxiety, focussing instead on the role of culture and interpersonal relationships. Horney proposed a model in which an adverse family environment — for example, a home with disturbed interpersonal relationships — causes 'basic anxiety', which is her term for anxiety based on feeling alone and helpless in a hostile world. The basic need underlying basic anxiety, according to Horney, isn't for some kind of instinctual expression (as per Freud), but for security, and it leads children to develop self-defeating strategies of defence.

Horney suggests that what Freud calls instinctual drives — such as aggression — are themselves a product of anxiety. Freud's concept of drive implies a compulsion from within, but according to Horney (*Neurosis and Human Growth: The Struggle Towards Self-Realisation*), drives are impulses and needs that stem from anxiety:

> When we call a drive compulsive we mean the opposite of spontaneous wishes or strivings. The latter are an expression of the real self; the former are determined by the inner necessities of the neurotic structure. The individual must abide by them regardless of his real wishes, feelings, or interests lest he incur anxiety, feel torn by conflicts, be overwhelmed by guilt feelings, feel rejected by others, etc. In other words, the difference between spontaneous and compulsive is one between 'I want' and 'I must in order to avoid some danger'.

So much for Freud's Eros and Thanatos. In Horney's system, we don't have an inherently destructive instinct. We can certainly become self-destructive or violent towards others, but this doesn't just happen, or emerge from a wish to return to an 'inorganic state' (as Freud reasoned). Any compulsion, or strident, demanding need, says Horney, comes from an interpersonal issue that has caused anxiety.

Whether or not we possess autonomous destructive and sexual drives has significant implications for what we can expect out of life and ourselves. Freud's system has a decidedly pessimistic tone, because it assumes that our aggressive and sexual instincts will always be in conflict with the demands of a civilised society. Even the majesty contained in works of art are simply forms of sublimation in Freud's eyes, ways we have channelled biological drives related to sex and aggression into acceptable containers. The most we can hope for in this life is to swap 'neurotic unhappiness' for 'common unhappiness' and get on with the daily grind, living a life of compromise.

Horney paints a more hopeful picture, in which there is no necessary conflict between civilisation and human nature, because there is no innate autonomous destructive instinct. Instead, the grounds for aggression lie in interpersonal relations and poor environmental conditions: if our basic needs for safety and satisfaction aren't met, we become unhappy, defensive and destructive.

The environmental factors that matter the most in the generation of basic anxiety are conditions in the family that make a child feel unsafe, unloved and unvalued. And as we'll see shortly, Horney's theory of defences stems from her own experience in a volatile household, and with a favoured sibling.

Just a Girl: Horney's Early Years

Karen Danielsen was born in Hamburg in 1885. Her father, Berndt ('Wackels'), was a sea captain and her mother, Clothilde ('Sonni'), was the daughter of a successful architect. Wackels was forty-four and a widower with four nearly grown children when he married Sonni, who was then twenty-eight. Karen was the second of two children born to the couple, the first being her brother Berndt, born four years before her.

SEEING THE PROBLEM AS IT IS—PART I: KAREN HORNEY'S DEFENSIVE...

The marriage wasn't a happy one. Wackels spent a lot of time at sea and the relative peace of the household was always disturbed when he returned home. Wackels had a temper, and Karen and her brother always sided with Sonni against 'the Bible Thrower' — a nickname the children gave Wackels for his tendency to literally throw the Bible. Sonni was the long-suffering wife; pleasant and popular amongst the locals. Karen's teenage diaries give a clear picture of both her sympathies and animosities at the time:

> I'm often quite sad and discouraged. For things are bad at home, and Mutti [Sonni], my all, is so ill and unhappy. Oh, how I would love to help her and cheer her up.
>
> It must be grand to have a father one can love and esteem, and when the 4th Commandment does not confront one like a terrifying specter [sic] with its 'thou shalt _____'. I can't do it. I can't respect that man who makes us all unhappy with his dreadful hypocrisy, selfishness, crudeness, and ill-breeding, etc.

Teenage Karen certainly gives her father a hard review, yet other reports suggest that Karen had great admiration for her father when she was a child, and talked about him with awe. Even more the painful, then, when Wackels refused to let Karen attend studies at university. Sonni, aware of her daughter's intellectual ability as a potential source of family pride, intervened by putting in a good word for Karen with her father. For a time, Karen was left waiting in limbo, not knowing whether she would be granted her wish:

> This uncertainty makes me sick. Why can't Father make up his mind a little faster? He, who has flung out thousands for my stepbrother Enoch, who is both stupid and bad, first turns every additional penny he is to spend for me 10 times in his fingers. And we did make it clear to him that he has to feed me only as long as I

attend school. Once I have my diploma I most certainly don't want another penny from him. He would like me to stay at home now, so we could dismiss our maid and I could do her work. He brings me almost to the point of cursing my good gifts.

Karen felt that both her parents favoured her brother, Berndt (named after his father), for whom there had been no question about attending university. In all sorts of ways, Karen noticed her brother being treated differently to her, and she felt the injustice of it. Yet she didn't want to be an outsider in the home, so she developed admiration for her mother and brother and tried to please them to gain their acceptance. Despite her best efforts, however, Karen always felt left out of the brother–mother alliance. She noted in her diary, for example, that while her mother would simply let go of any harsh word from Berndt, she'd respond to the same from Karen with reproach.

Wackels was eventually persuaded by Sonni to let Karen attend university, and a short time later, when Karen was nineteen, Sonni and Wackels separated. There's no evidence of any further contact between Karen and her father. Karen felt abandoned by him, and at some stage, though the cause is unclear, she also felt rejected by her brother; Berndt made a point of not having much to do with her.

All of this sets the scene for a defensive system that Karen took on to satisfy her needs for security. Firstly, Sonni's hatred and open contempt for Wackels made Karen assume that aligning herself with Sonni would place her on the superior side. Karen modelled herself on her mother, repressed her resentment toward her and her brother and instead directed it all towards her father. She wanted to please Sonni and Berndt so she wouldn't be alone. She also developed what was to become a lifelong preoccupation: a fantasy of meeting a great man with whom she could merge, who would take care of her.

With her father's absence, her brother's rejection, and her suspicions of being second-best, Karen questioned whether she had really been wanted. The preference for boys in families was both obvious and long-standing throughout society, and is why one of Horney's major works is called *The Neurotic Personality of Our Time*. The neurotic personality is 'of our time' because it's influenced by the prevailing societal values, conditions, and opportunities.

Having modelled herself on her mother, yet finding a sacrificial life unsatisfying, Horney noted how society equated masochistic tendencies with 'feminine nature' and aggressive tendencies with 'masculine nature'. Rather than see either of these qualities as innately belonging to women or men, she regarded them as part of specific neurotic defensive structures designed to protect us from basic anxiety. Horney developed a theory that she regarded as gender-neutral, recognising that culture induces a greater frequency of some psychological defences and conflicts in men and others in women. These defences are the subject of Part Two of this chapter, along with an examination of them in light of *A Course in Miracles*.

Seeing the Problem as It Is—Part II: Karen Horney's Defensive Solutions

According to Horney, basic anxiety arises out of an inner conflict between dependency and hostility: between feeling dependent on our parents and experiencing anger towards them. 'Regular' anxiety is experienced if our needs aren't met — for example, a need for food — but this can also make us hostile. Since we depend on our parents for everything when we are children — for physical, emotional and psychological comfort — we don't want to damage our relationship with them by venting our hostility. Yet, keeping our feelings under wraps doesn't help us a great deal, because the hostility will remain and make us feel guilty and fearful of reprisal. This in turn leads to basic anxiety, along with feelings of weakness.

Horney points out that it's not deprivation or punishment per se that is the problem in basic anxiety, but the spirit in which it occurs. If a child feels rejected, unwanted, unsafe, confused by mixed messages, or displaced by another child, their anxiety can lead to the development of neurotic defences.

Neurotic defences can form a pattern — a particular structure resembling a personality — that functions as a form of armour. We adopt it to keep us safe but it also alienates us from our true self. Therefore, we can't help but still feel lonely on some level, for the self we've left behind. We limit our self-expression, spontaneity and preferences in order to adjust to our chosen armour.

Horney's Defensive Solutions

Horney identified three major patterns of neurotic defences to basic anxiety, and she called these patterns 'solutions': the compliant, aggressive, and detached solutions. Each represents a movement *towards*, *against* and *away* from others respectively.

The compliant person moves towards others in an attempt to cling to the most powerful person around them. They protect themselves from a fear of retribution by becoming submissive and not upsetting people, and have an idealised view of love in which a perfect match would solve all their problems and provide them with ultimate fulfilment. They fear expressing personal power in the world and challenging authority, are self-effacing, self-sacrificial, and prone to stretch themselves way too thin in their desire to please and help others. Their driving need is for affection and be thought of as a good person: they have, what is commonly called these days, a 'disease to please'.

The aggressive person moves against others by rebelling and fighting. They react against their own feelings of helplessness and inferiority by striving for power and control over others. They like people to be envious of them, they're happy to exploit others to get to the top, and they generally have what we'd now call a narcissistic personality. And no matter how strong the cliché, I still come across people with this solution citing *My Way* as their favourite song. While the compliant type is afraid of upsetting or displeasing people, the aggressive type is afraid of feeling insignificant. (Horney also describes three sub-sets of the aggressive type, a full description of which can be found in my book *Above the Battleground: the Courageous Path to Emotional Autonomy and Inner Peace*.)

Horney identifies the craving for affection (the compliant solution) and the craving for power and control (the aggressive solution) as the two main driving forces in the adoption of neurotic defences. The compliant type needs to feel they are a good person, and the aggressive type needs to feel they are significant. In terms of *A Course in Miracles*, we can see these two solutions as reflecting the two main ways we can respond to the perceived split from God.

The compliant type is fearful of God's retaliation for moving independently (a challenge to His authority); the aggressive type feels abandoned/rejected by God (a projection of their own act of turning their back on God's Love, saying it wasn't enough) and fears being regarded as inferior or insignificant.

> All who believe in separation have a basic fear of retaliation and abandonment. They believe in attack and rejection, so that is what they perceive and teach and learn.[48]

In line with the work of psychoanalyst Helen Block Lewis on shame and guilt proneness, we can equate the compliant type with guilt-proneness, and the aggressive type with shame-proneness. And of course, societal expectations and conditioning surrounding gender means that each of these types tends to be exhibited more or less along those lines. The guilt-prone person is concerned with doing the right thing; the shame-prone person with doing something impressive (good or bad).

Whether you adopt the compliant or the aggressive solution, you will still feel a great deal of ups and downs according to how your defensive needs are met: both solutions rely heavily on your interactions with others. Horney's third solution is an attempt to avoid this emotional turmoil, and is called the detached solution. The detached person moves away from others by trying to shut them out of their inner life, withdrawing from them emotionally. The main desire of the detached person is not to be bothered by people. They don't want to feel tied down by others or restricted in any way. Getting to know people can lead to expectations and demands; better to stay detached and be free, cruising through life on an even keel.

Having adopted a solution to defend us from basic anxiety, believing that this behavioural pattern will keep us safe, we're now faced with another problem: any threat to this pattern becomes anxiety-producing. If a situation arises that requires us to act in a way that challenges our usual mode of relating to others, we feel threatened.

For example, the compliant/dependent type might fear that if they are assertive, their partner will leave them or retaliate in some other way. Or, if a person's safety depends on being unobtrusive, anxiety will emerge when they are thrust into the limelight. In contrast, the aggressive type — whose basic anxiety as a child could be allayed by admiration — will experience anxiety at the prospect of being unrecognised and unadmired.

Horney believed that a great deal of therapeutic effect lies in simply becoming aware of your defensive patterns. We can become aware of the past shaping our attitude, but there's real benefit in being able to place that attitude within a larger constellation of defences and seeing the logic behind the whole. By understanding the function of an attitude ('I have to please'; 'Being noticed is important'), we are better able to distance ourselves from it, taking on the position of an observer. For example, we can say how our need for affection clashes with someone's need to dominate and control, and why we truly hate each other in those moments. In Course terms, we can see how our special love bargains — in which we'll scratch someone's solution if they'll scratch ours — turn into opportunities for hostility when we don't get our security needs met.

Defences: A Double-Edged Sword

Apart from adopting her mother's compliant solution to a large degree, Karen Horney also recognised she had a need to become something special, and that this stemmed from inferiority feelings, most likely in relation to the status of her brother within the family, and to her feelings of abandonment. Academic achievement was a way of compensating for this sense of inferiority and fear of further abandonment. However, her strong sense of ambition went against the grain of her compliant solution, which demanded that she be self-effacing, modest, and concerned with pleasing others. This caused so much inner conflict that Horney experienced a recurring paralysing fatigue that inhibited her ability to work.

That's the thing with adopting a defensive solution: the tendencies of the opposite solution remain within us, and the tension between them means that we can never really proceed with anything in a wholehearted way. Readers familiar with Carl Jung's work will see the similarity between Horney's conflicting solutions and Jung's theory on reconciling opposites. What Jung regards as projections of the anima and animus — the disowned feminine and masculine within — shares a lot in common with Horney's compliant and aggressive types respectively. The solution we abhor in another (aggressive dominance and selfishness, for example, or fastidiousness and fussing over others,) shows us what we have disowned within ourselves. The task is to forgive ourselves for those very qualities and in the process allow the positive equivalents (self-expression and self-care; thoroughness and being considerate) to come through.

We can also view the aggressive and compliant solutions with regard to the Course's use of 'leader' and 'follower' respectively:

> The leader and the follower emerge as separate roles, each seeming to possess advantages you would not want to lose. So in their fusion there appears to be the hope of satisfaction and of peace. You see yourself divided into both these roles, forever split between the two...
>
> Perhaps you call it love. Perhaps you think that it is murder justified at last. You hate the one you gave the leader's role when you would have it, and you hate as well his not assuming it at times you want to let the follower in you arise, and give away the role of leadership.[49]

Leader and follower, hammer and anvil, victimiser and victim. Whichever we choose to identify with, we'll experience loss because we've identified with differences and therefore with separation. Healing occurs when we choose to walk beside someone in acknowledgement of our common need — to know of our holy Self.

Becoming aware of our defences is an important first step in getting to know when we've chosen the ego. Without the Holy Spirit's help, however, the task of letting them go is too great because we're so identified with the world's dream and with the body. Our sense of insecurity can only be surmounted by exchanging our perspective for a view from 'above the battleground' where we know of the wholeness and invulnerability of our spiritual Self.

The Solutions don't succeed in defending us from a fear of punishment/calamity (guilt) and from a fear of abandonment and sense of incompletion (shame). This is because our fear of retaliation and abandonment ultimately stems from our belief that we have separated from God: we first felt a need to defend ourselves when we believed we had accomplished the impossible and attacked God's Oneness by usurping His role as authority and turning our back on His Love. We now fear abandonment, rejection, retaliation and calamity whenever we identify with the ego thought system. We then run to our defensive solutions for help, but as we've seen, this only prolongs and intensifies our pain:

> Yet is defensiveness a double threat. For it attests to weakness, and sets up a system of defence that cannot work. Now are the weak still further undermined, for there is treachery without and still a greater treachery within. The mind is now confused, and knows not where to turn to find escape from its imaginings.[50]

By going straight to our defensive solutions when we perceive a threat, we are reinforcing our vulnerability instead of diminishing it. Not only do we perceive a threat outside of us, but we feel a threat inside in the form of an inherent weakness. This sets up a vicious cycle in which seeking affirmations from outside ourselves makes us feel weaker inside, which in turn makes us feel the need for more external affirmation… and on it goes. The very existence of a defence says that we have chosen to believe that we have separated from God, which is why they are 'the costliest of all the prices which the ego would exact'.[51]

This vicious cycle ramps up the intensity of our demands on someone or something outside ourselves to alleviate our anxiety. And of course, nothing is quite so off-putting than someone else's neediness; this is particularly so for the aggressive and detached solutions. All the more important, then, for a compliant type to remember to ask for help from the Holy Spirit to look at what is going on when they feel anxious and in need of external affirmations to feel safe. So too for the aggressive type who finds themselves feeling a lack of power or control; and for the detached type who is forced through circumstance to develop a degree of intimacy with others, such as during a time of illness.

In every situation in which we feel unsure of our worth and our security, we can remember to choose between the weakness of our ego and its defences, and the strength of our one Self (Christ) in us:

> Defencelessness is strength. It testifies to recognition of the Christ in you. Perhaps you will recall the text maintains that choice is always made between Christ's strength and your own weakness, seen apart from Him...[52]

We are not alone and helpless in a hostile world. At least, we don't have to perceive things this way, and we won't perceive them this way if we remember who walks with us, and that our safety lies in the truth of our wholeness and holiness.

In the Course's Workbook Lesson 37, 'My holiness blesses the world', we are told that our purpose and true function is to see the world through our own holiness. If we look through the eyes of our ego and thus with our defensive system, we will feel we need something from someone else in order to feel good/powerful/free/secure. In contrast, 'Those who see themselves as whole make no demands'. Of course, this refers to content and not form: our requests needn't come from emotional neediness.

A sense of peace and contentment follows our decision to identify with our holiness and strength. It is a feeling of self-respect and wholeness, in recognition of our shared Self. We belong to ourselves rather than to our ego and the tyranny of our defensive solution's 'shoulds' and 'musts', and can rest inwardly no matter what we are doing. You could say that an aim of the Course is to help us carry this sense of rest with us, in recognition that there's nothing we need do for our salvation because our Self is just perfect, right here, right now, as it is.

> Your holiness is the answer to every question that was ever asked, is being asked now, or will be asked in the future. Your holiness means the end of guilt, and therefore the end of hell.[53]

Anxiety, Hostility and Unconditional Love

Listening to a podcast recently, I heard a scenario that sounded all too familiar. A woman who usually went holidaying overseas on her own decided to take her grandson along. The problem was that ever since the trip had been booked she'd been anxious about it. She couldn't pin down the source of the anxiety; she only knew that she wasn't looking forward to it as she always did when she'd planned to travel on her own.

In such cases, I find psychological theory to be very helpful in applying the principles of *A Course in Miracles*. Psychoanalyst Karen Horney maintained that hostility was beneath many experiences of anxiety, and that it related to feelings of dependency. If we feel dependent on the approval of others for emotional security, we'll also hate those people in moments when we really don't want to comply with their expectation or request. The searing question in those moments is 'Can I do what *I* want and still get the approval I crave in order to feel secure?' If we decide that the answer is no, we get angry, suppress it, and it comes out as anxiety.

For the woman in the above scenario, the need to be 'good' and please her grandson had most likely tipped her over the edge in terms of a people-pleasing attitude she had adopted to get by in the world. In the past, she might have been grateful for the opportunity to please someone, thus gaining the approval she felt she needed. Now, something in her was saying 'Enough!' Hence the anxiety and underlying anger.

This reminds me of a time I was at the beach, watching a boy about four years old play delightedly within the shallow fringe of the water. Two adults approached him — I assumed they were his grandparents — and told him it was time to go home. He pretended not to hear them and continued playing. After several attempts to coax him out with gentle words, the grandfather lifted him up and began carrying him away, saying 'There, you're a good boy'. The boy, crying, said defiantly, 'But I don't *want* to be a good boy!' And I think that sums it up. Why be good when you could be happy? This is the question that emerges when people for whom self-sacrifice is a way of life finally snap.

The thing about the overseas holiday example is that the woman's relationship with her grandson might have been the same whether she'd asked him to join her on the trip or not. Her identification with guilt was so strong, that she inadvertently created a scenario in which she felt she had to sacrifice her happiness to please someone else.

On the other side of the spectrum, someone who feels a competitive need to excel in their chosen field may one day feel the anxiety and hostility behind feeling driven to succeed. Why do they have to achieve so much in order to be loved, significant, secure? In both examples, anxiety is the expression of a hostility that says to others, 'Your love/support/care shouldn't be conditional!'

But of course, all love in this world is conditional when we have identified with the ego. If I condemn you for the conditions that I imagine you place on your love, then I'm also condemning myself for my own conditions. When we identify with the ego, we identify with lack and vulnerability. We therefore seek to get from others what we feel is lacking in ourselves. These are the 'special relationships' *A Course in Miracles* talks about: you'll get a special something from me to reassure you of your goodness or worth, and you should return the favour. This is the 'special love bargain'. If you don't return the favour, then I am entitled to hate you.

When we realise how we've strived for a sense of security based on guilt and shame, we have a chance to forgive ourselves for having chosen such an unholy self-concept. If someone is demanding that we do something we don't really want to do, and this makes us anxious, then that's a sure sign we have chosen to identify with our ego and adopt a 'one or the other' mentality — someone must lose in order for someone else to gain. Anxiety can also be accompanied by depression; a belief in conditional love means we'll experience a sense of loss for God's unconditional Love.

If we don't want to do what a defensive strategy usually has us doing (pleasing, achieving), the answer is to go within and ask for help to remember that our holiness is our salvation, and nothing else. Then, whatever we do or don't do will come from a place of wholeness rather than scarcity, and everyone will gain from our peace that is the outcome. But, as always, half the battle in putting such principles into practice is remembering to do it!

Play School: The World as Transitional Object

I can't imagine Charlie Brown's friend Linus without his blanket; the two are inextricably entwined. Linus is often pictured lovingly hugging his blanket close, or holding it whilst sucking his thumb. Likewise, many children develop strong attachments to a soft toy, a book, or just about any object. They take them everywhere, especially if they leave the house or experience unfamiliar circumstance or environments. These objects of comfort and security are what the British psychoanalyst and paediatrician Donald Winnicott called transitional objects, and they have an important function in the meeting of our internal and external worlds.

Transitional Objects

According to Winnicott, the transitional object is symbolic of a child's internal unity with a giving, accepting, nurturing parent. We first develop attachments to such objects between the ages four and twelve months as we begin to realise that we are separate from our mother or primary carer. In fact, because the child is trying to find a solution to the reality of their parent's separateness, that they can sometimes feel a greater need for the transitional object than the actual parent — they have some control over Blanket, Teddy or Buzz, but mum and dad come and go. And in less-than-ideal home environments, children can also begin to exercise an inner voice that is wise, understanding and supportive, with the help of a stuffed animal or other transitional object: 'No one understands me like Rabbit can', said a boy in one of Winnicott's studies.

As a child becomes accustomed to the reality of both their connectedness to others and their separateness, they gradually let go of their attachment to the transitional object — it's simply laid aside without fuss or the need for external encouragement. As adults we retain the habit of establishing special objects, such as a favourite mug, chair, or book, as symbols of the fusion we originally felt. Transitional objects are also replaced by transitional phenomena in the wider culture, such as music and works of art. A clear and literal example of art as transitional phenomena can be found in one of the world's largest sculptures, *Maman* by Louise Bourgeois. *Maman* is a steel sculpture of a spider-like creature measuring 30 ft high and 33 ft wide. It's an incredible work I find disconcerting and uncanny. For Bourgeoise, *Maman* evokes something entirely different, as expressed in her poem 'Ode to my Mother' (*Tate Modern*, 2000):

> The friend (the spider – why the spider?) because my best friend was my mother and she was deliberate, clever, patient, soothing, reasonable, dainty, subtle, indispensable, neat, and useful as an araignée. She could also defend herself, and me, by refusing to answer 'stupid', inquisitive, embarrassing personal questions.
>
> I shall never tire of representing her.

Likewise, some religious icons and beliefs can be regarded as transitional phenomena — the concept of God or Christ as a loving presence and a source of security can travel with us via a necklace with a cross; the promise of blessings from Ganesh can reach us through an image on the wall.

Transitional Space

The transitional object of the child occupies the transitional space between themselves and their parent. It is also the intermediate space between inner and outer worlds: between what is us and what is not us. Winnicott saw the transitional object — the cherished teddy bear, blanket, storybook — as something that a child sees as both 'not me' but also not 'not me'. What he meant was that while the object is something separate from the child, it is still within the child's control. It can respond to what they needed from it, they can pick it up when they choose to, and they can take it with them — in this sense, it is not 'not me'.

As adults, we can become particularly attached to objects that symbolise this meeting place between inner and outer worlds. Any creative pursuit, for example, involves a tangible meeting of inner and outer worlds. Just as I can't imagine Linus without his blanket, I always think of Charlie Brown's other friend Schroeder playing his piano. And then there's Peppermint Patty and her love of baseball, namely the sporting arena in which a significant aspect of her inner world is expressed. Chances are, Peppermint Patty had a significant attachment to her baseball mitt, and Schroeder to his piano. (Of course, Snoopy loved sleeping on top of his dog house, but I don't know that it qualifies as a transitional object.)

And then we have our heroes associated with our chosen field of endeavour. These heroes act as a kind of parent. Their strength is ours, their success our hope and inspiration, and their shared appreciation for our field makes them a source of understanding and care. They're our guides, our support, our comfort.

Whenever we come to a major threshold in life — a time of significant change, perhaps even turmoil — we can find ourselves unconsciously gravitating towards a hero (or two), and a transitional object which we both associate with them and with something essential to our own being. This was the case for Sophie Oliver, a university lecturer in English whose experience of pregnancy and motherhood was full of ambivalence.

Oliver detailed her experience in an essay, 'Jean Rhys's Dress' (*The Essay*,

BBC Radio 3, 2021), and describes how she felt ill equipped to mother a child. The whole pregnancy-motherhood scenario was totally different to anything she had known before, and she prized her independence. Not knowing who she was or what she was doing (the signature of being on edge of a threshold) she was drawn to a dress that was given to her by a friend, and that had belonged to the author Jean Rhys. Famous for her novel *Wide Sargasso Sea*, Rhys had also struggled with motherhood, and in later life rekindled a connection with her daughter through a mutual appreciation for clothes.

Oliver steeped herself in the world of Rhys — her novels and her personal life — and experienced a felt connection through Rhys's dress. The dress became Oliver's (self-described) 'transitional object', helping her connect with the world of literature which she loved and with a person, a hero, who had walked the path of motherhood before her and had managed. Just as the infant struggles with the dawning awareness of separation, mothers (and carers in general) can experience a loss of self in the all-consuming demands of their caretaker world. Rhys's dress was a tangible connection to the imagined mentorship of Rhys, and to the world of literature, which was an integral part of Oliver's sense of self.

In the transitional space, Oliver was able to retain a connection to what Winnicott calls the personal impulse, which helped her move toward a connection with her child. This might seem paradoxical, however Winnicott points out that we need to have a sense of our true self so that joining with another doesn't feel like a dangerous prospect, a potential loss of self. If we're caught up in finding and reacting to all sorts of impingements, then we have lost contact with our true self and personal impulse. The kind of pre-occupation that gets us frazzled — 'I have to do this! I have to do that! What should I do?!' — also has us feeling fragmented; without any sense of wholeness, confidence or stability. This is the stuff of a false self.

In contrast, our true self is a 'spontaneous expression of being'. According to Winnicott, the ideal is that we can 'be alone in the presence of others': that we are able to have a connection with the expansiveness and personal impulse of our true self whilst in company. In this way, we can interact without being reactive and defensive. We can be calm. Winnicott linked this to being able to tolerate the kind of mental expansiveness that is experienced through some meditative practices. We can let go of 'I, me and mine', if we feel connected to our true self.

If, as Jung says, the meaning of life is to embody the wholeness of our personality, then this process of meeting a threshold and discovering a transitional object might be central to growth. It's through a dialogue between our inner and outer worlds that we understand more about ourselves and how we co-exist with the rest of society. When we cross a threshold, we move from one classroom into another, and begin a new series of lessons, all designed to help us answer the question: What am I? To ask this question means being willing to recognise our defensiveness and our reactivity; our needs to please, appease, and control. What does our personal impulse say?

Play School

To Winnicott, being our true self means engaging with others in a spirit of reciprocity. In any relationship, reciprocity exists if we're not trying to impose something on someone (being aggressive), or submissively acquiescing in a spirit of defeat. Reciprocity implies an exchange in which all parties give and receive; there is a mutuality about it, instead of a sense of one-sidedness. This, according to Winnicott, naturally occurs when we are coming from our true self, as does an ability to be spontaneous, creative and playful. This is how our inner and outer worlds meet in a 'friendly' manner.

Creativity is the opposite of reactivity. The word 'creative' relates to something new, something beyond habit, beyond imitation; a surprise. There's no motive — to impose, to comply, to achieve — just a simple personal impulse to do whatever it is we do. Creativity begins when we trust ourselves enough to stop emulating our heroes (as supportive as they are) and start letting inspiration come through us. We emulate to learn, but then we must be prepared to put the books, written by our heroes, aside, and extend out our own antenna.

There is no great sense of 'I' in the truly creative space, no sense of competition, no battle to fight; these things place a limitation on the mind and obscure insight and spontaneity. Spontaneity isn't the same as compulsiveness or impulsiveness; there isn't a sense of being driven, or out of control. Spontaneity is, paradoxically, aliveness and relaxation at the same time. It is light and playful, and seeks nothing. If play becomes a competition, or requires meeting other people's expectations, it isn't play anymore. It isn't fun, or inherently rewarding.

The enjoyment of being engaged in play or creativity also means that life seems tedious when spontaneity ceases and we get back to 'the real world'. People who do what we generally regard as creative work — drawing, inventing, composing — often become depressed when they don't have a project to work on. If they're not engaged with their transitional object — the paintbrush, the piano, the typewriter — and bringing a creative impulse into fruition, life feels a lot heavier, duller.

The thing about inspiration is that it can't be forced. Your antenna might be up, but nothing's coming through — at least, not in a form that moves you to produce anything. You simply have to wait and keep that antenna up. However, depression and despondency dampen the connection. Not only do you feel down about not having a project to engage with, but your mood can lead to thoughts and ruminations (envy, anger, worry) that dull the antenna's receptivity. We might long for creativeness, but our very longing itself becomes an impediment, a perpetual source of disquiet. This is where it can be helpful (artist or not) to regard the whole world as a transitional object.

The World as Transitional Object

Workbook Lesson 29 in *A Course in Miracles* states 'God is in everything I see'. This doesn't mean that God is literally in everything, but that His purpose is:

> Certainly God is not in a table, for example, as you see it. Yet

we emphasised yesterday that a table shares the purpose of the universe.[54]

According to the Course's metaphysics, God didn't create the world, however He did place a memory of His Oneness within our minds, which the Course refers to as the Holy Spirit. God's purpose is forgiveness — our pathway to remembering the innocence and wholeness of our spiritual Self. Seeing God's purpose in everything we see means giving it the purpose of remembering our Self, instead of reinforcing guilt and shame and a host of grievances.

A particular chair, for example, might remind us of who sat in it regularly, and this might bring up a load of unhappy memories. Or perhaps you see a chair in a shop that you'd love to buy but can't afford, and this leads to a spiral of resentments based on feelings of 'not enough' — not enough money, not enough power, not enough love when you were younger, not enough attention… *not enough.* When we see through the lens of the past and the ego, we don't see anything as it is now, we don't see it with vision.

The whole world can become our transitional object if we choose to see God's purpose within it:

> Try then, today, to begin to learn how to look on all things with love, appreciation and open-mindedness. You do not see them now. Would you know what is in them? Nothing is as it appears to you. Its holy purpose stands beyond your little range. When vision has shown you the holiness that lights up the world, you will understand today's idea perfectly.[55]

A transitional object is something that reminds us of an inner source of security and comfort, and at the same time helps our personal impulse emerge within our relationships. What I mean by personal impulse, is the creative impulse that isn't based on preconceived ideas about ourselves and others, that doesn't come from defensiveness, and that doesn't have a 'Here we go again…' moan attached to it. When we're identified with our ego, our reactive impulse — associated with a false self — is given free rein. We translate everything in terms of our accumulated experience, our prejudices and expectations. Whatever we do from this place will be old. If we're coming from a need to gain, or to avoid loss, then we're in this mindset, and nothing we do can truly be regarded as creative.

To live a creative life really means to see creative opportunities all around us, all of the time. Life itself becomes playful as we meet each circumstance with the desire to extend our antenna and be receptive to having a new response where previously we could only ever imagine the same, dull, tiresome reaction; a sigh, a cry, a compulsive need to fix something. This is the time to see our Inner Teacher's purpose in the world, to call on Them for help, and to extend our antenna. Our judgements will fade as we observe them, and from this place of observation that is without 'I, me or mine', there can be perpetual renewal. This is true creativity.

The Only True Reflection

> She will have her own version. I am not the centre of her story, because she herself is that. But I could give her something you can never have, except from another person: what you look like from outside. A reflection. This is part of herself I could give back to her.
> — Margaret Atwood, Cat's Eye

Minding our neighbour's small dog Kimba one evening, I was amused at his reaction to an image of a koala crawling across the television screen. Kimba's eyes lit up and he ran towards the iconic Australian marsupial, then followed it as it moved out of shot. The koala nowhere to be seen, Kimba looked behind the television. No koala there. Bemused, Kimba continued searching for the magical disappearing creature until eventually giving up and resuming his position on his day-bed.

What I'd taken for granted for so many years — that what's on the television screen isn't actually happening, *right there* — was something Kimba had never learnt. Perhaps this relates to the fact that dogs can't recognise their reflection. This ability is unique to only a few species, including humans, some great apes, and possibly dolphins, elephants and magpies.

Human infants don't recognise their own reflection until they're about eighteen months of age. Until then, if you put a bit of lipstick (or rouge in the Seventies, when this test was developed) onto the infant's nose then place them in front of a mirror, they won't show any reaction apart from smiling and trying to play with the baby looking back at them. Around eighteen months, babies begin to show signs of noticing the lipstick. They can appear slightly distressed, and try to rub the lipstick off their own nose.

Recognising ourselves in a mirror involves being able to perceive ourselves as an independent being. We look in the mirror and register 'that is me'. It's a sign of developing a sense of self; of being a unified being rather than just part of a landscape of happenings. We become conscious that we're an 'I' amongst others. And as the 'I' comes more into conscious awareness, we literally become self-conscious; now what happens to us, happens to an 'I', an identity, and it is taken personally. We develop emotions such as empathy, pride and guilt, which are all based on an ability to make comparisons.

According to psychoanalyst Donald Winnicott, a sense of 'I' begins developing before infants can recognise themselves in a mirror. We start discovering ourselves by what is mirrored to us — reflected about us — through the faces of our parents or primary carers. The conscious identity is thereby formed slowly, leading up to being able to recognise ourselves in a mirror. The gaze of the carer reflects the carer's perception of the baby, contributing to their sense of self through an 'I–Thou' relationship.

Being able to recognise our reflection isn't just a sign of developmental progress, but leads to what the French psychoanalyst Jacques Lacan suggested is something of a shock. According to Lacan, the mirror stage can be very unsettling because the face we see doesn't necessarily look the way we feel. We experience so much flux internally — there's a constant stream of speeding thoughts and feelings, new sensations and desires. Inside, we are all over the place, but our reflection shows something stable, something clearly defined. As we grow older, the disjunction between our inner world and our outer appearance is experienced as an existential dilemma: how can we accurately convey what is inside us to others? An image doesn't communicate our self, and words are hardly adequate to describe all that we feel and comprehend. How on earth can we avoid being misunderstood?

Celebrities experience the trappings of this inner-outer miscommunication all the time — they are not the image they portray, or the characters they play. I remember a friend who'd attended many Twelve Step meetings saying, 'Don't judge someone's insides from their outsides'. She'd seen it all, and she knew the truth of that statement. Alas, though we long for others to understand us deeply, people will often be resolutely stuck on our exterior, assuming us to be pretty much what we seem and interpreting everything we do and say accordingly. With misunderstanding comes loneliness; we can try and convey who we are through managing our appearance or publicising our likes and dislikes, but no one will ever experience us the way we experience ourselves and vice versa.

This reminds me of lyrics from Kate Bush's song 'Running Up That Hill (A Deal with God)':

> And if I only could
> I'd make a deal with God
> And I'd get him to swap our places

In an interview with Richard Skinner (BBC Radio 1, 1992), Bush explained that the song emerged from a 'What if?' thought about swapping places with your partner so you could properly understand each other. Both parties would likely be surprised, and perhaps would get along better afterwards.

What's Inside

Though each of us is unique in body and psychological make-up, yearning to be understood, what is essential to us in terms of our greatest fears and greatest need is the same. *A Course in Miracles* makes it clear that all of our distress comes from a belief that we have separated from God and made a substitute world in which we live an autonomous existence. Attached to our experience of self in the world is the idea of sin — of having destroyed our Creator's Oneness and turned our back on His all-encompassing Love. 'Destroyer of Love', that's what we think we are. That is the self-concept that never lets us rest, relax or feel at peace. Indeed, the Course's psychotherapy pamphlet states: 'And who could weep but for his innocence?' (P-2.IV.1:7). The offender we curse outside of us — the fiend, the felon, the object of scorn — shares our name:

> You think you are the home of evil, darkness and sin. You think if anyone could see the truth about you he would be repelled, recoiling from you as if from a poisonous snake.[56]

It's some consolation at least to know everyone believes this about themselves, though we cover it over with a range of defences. We become the successful person, the helpful person, the unassuming one, the cheery one, the entertainer — you name it. There's a relatively innocuous identity for everyone, and none would suspect the enormity of what lies beneath. No one could live with the magnitude of guilt associated with believing we attacked God without these defences; in terms of staying alive, it's a job well done. We build a nice idea of ourselves, even if it's lowly in parts, and we project our underlying guilt outwards, seeing it in others and condemning it there. In this respect, the world becomes a mirror for the guilt within our minds. It is a 'darkened glass', showing us only the darkness of the ego's world, its purpose dominating our perception:

> The darkened glass the world presents can show but twisted images in broken parts. The real world pictures Heaven's innocence.[57]

> When your mood tells you that you have chosen wrongly, and this is so whenever you are not joyous, then know this need not be. In every case you have thought wrongly about some brother God created, and are perceiving images your ego makes in a darkened glass.[58]

Because we believe we rejected God, and now fear retaliation, we'll fear and perceive rejection and retaliation all around us — whether it's there or not. Our guilt-anxiety produces the Chicken Little effect, in which we fear catastrophe around every corner. Shame-anxiety, or fear of rejection and abandonment, makes us sensitive to people ignoring us, belittling us or treating us with contempt. We'll also be on the lookout for people we can project our sense of inferiority onto. Though we might belong to a minority group or otherwise be marginalised, we can revel in finding someone lower down in the pecking-order onto whom we can cast our disdain. Our perceptions of the world are full of comparisons regarding value and power, and a lot of our mental life is occupied with trying to locate ourselves on the scale.

Beyond this shame and guilt-laden self-concept is the memory of our holiness. Our spiritual Self remains unaffected by our belief in sin and unworthiness, even while its memory is obscured by our grievances and judgements:

> Earth can reflect Heaven or hell; God or the ego. You need but leave the mirror clean and clear of all the images of hidden darkness you have drawn upon it. God will shine upon it of Himself.[59]

While the world mirrors back to us what we believe about ourselves, these beliefs — looked at from a developmental perspective — can be traced to what was mirrored to us by primary carers and society as a whole when we were children. Though from the perspective of the Course's myth and metaphysics, it's our belief in having separated from God that is the cause of our poor self-concept, from a developmental perspective it all starts at home. For example, the parent that routinely meets us with a disapproving gaze, or ignores us altogether, has a potent effect on our sense of self. Who could argue otherwise? As maker of the world, the ego has designed childhood to be the perfect set-up for establishing a poor self-concept and one in which we feel victim to a cruel world.

The Course's path of forgiveness doesn't involve skipping over our worldly experiences of victimhood and abuse in order to remember the holiness and innocence of our spiritual Self. It uses these experiences to help us get back to base in a gentle and kind way that allows us to forgive the people we believe to be responsible for our feelings of unworthiness. The process of forgiveness is the Course's indirect means of remembering our unity with God and the wholeness of our Self.

The ways in which our lowly self-concept is expressed shows the world a picture of our victimisation. There's that classic line from Mary Shelley's *Frankenstein* when the creature says to his maker: 'I was benevolent and good; misery made me a fiend.' The creature's accusation was that because Dr Frankenstein hadn't created a companion for him, and people turned away from him in terror and disgust, he was left to endure a life of alienation, and it was *this* that made him act out against society and hurt all whom the doctor loved:

> Remember that I am thy creature; I ought to be thy Adam, but I am rather the fallen angel, whom thou drivest from joy for no misdeed. Everywhere I see bliss, from which I alone am irrevocably excluded.

The crimes of the creature were an indictment of his creator. And so it is with all of us. There will be certain people, a 'special few', who we blame for our lowly self-concept and our unkindness (towards ourselves or others). Through practicing forgiveness, the peace in our minds that takes the place of our grievances shows these objects of our hate that they too aren't the monstrous creature they might think they are:

> In this world you can become a spotless mirror, in which the

Holiness of your Creator shines forth from you to all around you.[60]

Could you but realise for a single instant the power of healing that the reflection of God, shining in you, can bring to all the world, you could not wait to make the mirror of your mind clean to receive the image of the holiness that heals the world... All bring their different problems to its healing light, and all their problems find but healing there.[61]

My own need to see my innocence reflected in another's gaze was brought home to me in a dream I had several years ago. I dreamt I was standing in the kitchen of my childhood home, having an argument with two people standing opposite me. I became infuriated by a comment I felt was personally demeaning. I totally lost it. I screamed something in retaliation then picked up a nearby ceramic mug and violently hurled it towards them. They ducked out of the way just in time then met me with startled yet indignant gazes which seemed to say, 'We can't believe anyone would do such a horrible thing!' I instantly felt sick with dread. At that moment, I noticed someone else standing in the room. It was my father. I looked at him, expecting to see a similar look of outrage on his face, but instead was met with the most serene, loving and accepting expression — as if nothing at all had happened. A wave of relief passed through me. I was so grateful. 'Come on', he said. 'Isn't it time to take me home now?'

It was a touching dream. When I was a child, my father represented that face of terrible disapproval, and I felt it acutely. My sensitivity to put-downs in the dream symbolised a lack of self-worth that I could attribute to my father's treatment. 'Isn't it time to take me home now?' meant isn't it time I let go of the poor-self-worth issue? Could I forgive my father ('take him home') so I might be a mirror of his innocence just as he, in the dream, was one for me?

> Clean but the mirror, and the message that shines forth from what the mirror holds out for everyone to see, no one can fail to understand. It is the message that the Holy Spirit is holding to the mirror that is in him. He recognizes it because he has been taught his need for it, but knows not where to look to find it. Let him, then, see it in you and share it with you.[62]

We all have a need to know we are worthy, innocent, whole. We all need a reminder of Who it is we really are. We don't need to swap bodies in order to understand each other or communicate effectively, we just need to decide whether we want to see innocence or guilt when we look out onto the world. If truth is our goal, then no matter what someone does, we will perceive it as either a call for help (if it appears to be an attack) or an expression of love. Either way, our response will be to let go of judgement and meet them with kindness: to reflect back to them their holiness in recognition that they don't have the power to take the peace of God away from us. No harm done. This is true communication, without the neediness of our ego that is full of demands and investments which obscure vision.

Our tolerance for pain isn't without limit. Though we are attached to our separate ego identity, we eventually realise it's fool's gold. There's no happiness there, no great reward. When we finally choose the Holy Spirit as our teacher and learn the value of forgiveness, we begin to see and reflect innocence, and God's Creation is mirrored in the world:

> Christ's vision is a Miracle. It comes from far beyond itself, for it reflects eternal love and the rebirth of love which never dies, but has been kept obscure. Christ's vision pictures Heaven, for it sees a world so like to Heaven that what God created perfect can be mirrored there.[63]

In the Shadow of Gods—Part I: On Human Frailty and Self-Doubt

I recently read *How to Be Invisible*, a book of lyrics by Kate Bush. Reading David Mitchell's foreword, I came across the answer to a question I had harboured for many years: what was the inspiration for the music video to 'Cloudbusting'? The video features Bush, short-haired and wearing overalls, helping a towering older man (Canadian actor Donald Sutherland) wheel a large, strange contraption up a hill in the countryside. You soon figure out the machine is a 'cloudbuster' for bringing on rain. The drama kicks in as several men dressed in black drive towards the mountain, later apprehending Sutherland and taking him away in their car. Bush runs wide-eyed and desperate down the hill towards them, tumbling and scrambling on the way. The video is moving for its portrayal of childhood devotion.

The song 'Cloudbusting' is based on the memoir, *A Book of Dreams*, written by Peter Reich, the son of psychoanalyst and inventor, Wilhelm Reich. I was familiar with the father, but not the son, and that in itself speaks to the heart of the memoir. Wilhelm Reich had a strong personality, and made a name for himself with the publication of his book *Character Analysis* in 1933. Reich emphasised the effects of emotional conflicts and trauma on the musculature of the body: we develop 'muscular armouring' in response to our conflicts, and undoing the armouring through therapeutic breathing exercises can free us of these conflicts.

There's little controversy around Reich's theory of character types and associated musculature armouring — many therapies today incorporate it.

Later in life, however, Reich went on to develop a theory of 'life energy' based on sexuality, and invented an Orgone Accumulator, a metal box in which you could sit and absorb 'orgone energy', which Reich claimed cured all sorts of physical ailments. Reich sold these boxes, placing him in conflict with the American Food and Drug Administration, which led to his arrest and imprisonment.

Reich was consumed with the idea of energy — energy within the body, energy in the atmosphere, energy anywhere and everywhere. Convinced that aliens were directing invisible energy attacks towards earth from UFOs, he invented a space gun to neutralise the attacks. And as Bush's video depicts, Reich also claimed to be able to make rain using his cloudbusting machine which propelled cloud dispersing energy into the sky. In all of these pursuits, Reich's young son Peter was his loyal, adoring soldier at arms, soaking up everything his father said as the truth about things, and admiring Wilhelm's loyal following of maverick scientists. For thirteen years, until his father died, Peter was a 'Cosmic Engineer', a lieutenant in his dad's army, ready to do battle to defend the work of his father and promote the truth.

Towards the end of Peter's memoir, there's a reckoning with his past. He realises that his father's obsession had left his own needs, his own self, on the sidelines. Everything revolved around his father's work and talent. Peter's mother was also a scientist and worked alongside Wilhelm, but she too felt the effects of Reich's obsession; everyone was subsumed by Reich's projects. She eventually left.

Later, as an adult, the effects of his father's dominance hit home. One night, Peter met a woman a bar. On the cusp of becoming intimate with him, she paused, explaining her hesitation by saying she didn't yet know who he was. His reaction betrayed a life in his father's shadow: 'I'm Wilhelm Reich's son', he said, without thinking. And as soon as he'd said it, he knew he was wrong: 'I felt the scream rising within me, a scream that left me spinning and falling alone, lost in space'.

Moving from an identity as 'Wilhelm Reich's son' to being himself involved Peter acknowledging his father's limitations. His father wasn't a god; he loved his son, but he also had failings. Like all of us, Wilhelm Reich was a mixed bag. As an adult, Peter was able to look at his father through different eyes, however he was torn by a sense of loyalty to him. Peter had shifted in his view of Wilhelm as the ultimate authority. When, for example, Reich told his son that people were out to get him — that if he went to prison, he would be killed — thirteen-year-old Peter believed him. However, when his father died whilst incarcerated, Peter wondered if the true cause of death was really heart failure, as officially reported.

It's evident from Peter's memoir that his father had for a long time suffered from a chronic heart condition, but Reich never disclosed this to Peter, instead perpetuating the idea that he'd die in prison at the hands of people who knew of the importance of his work and were afraid of it. As an adult, Peter wondered if it would be unfaithful to his father to no longer believed his conspiracy theories. Loyalty demanded that he retain the child's perspective of things if his father was to remain a god. The choice seemed to be between seeing his father as a god or as a charlatan. But he was neither: he was simply human.

Peter's story puts the 'parent-as-God' scenario into stark relief. Our stories mightn't be as clear-cut or dramatic, but all of us first make our parents into objects of worship, losing something of ourselves in the process. Later we need to come to terms with their humanity. The giving up of the mythological, god-like images of our parents is, however, resisted well into adulthood. We harbour a hope that they can give us something that we desperately need. What that something is and why we feel we need it is the subject of the following discussion. We begin by looking at how the ego's world has been set up for the creation of demi-gods, and how the principles of *A Course in Miracles* can help us put things into perspective, promoting healing.

Half-Baked: Our Humble Beginnings

Compared to birds and mammals, newborn reptiles are particularly independent creatures. Take a sea turtle, for example. The pregnant female crawls out of the surf and up the beach till she reaches above the high-water mark.

There she digs a hole in the sand with her flippers into which she lays her eggs, then covers them with sand. With this last act of maternal care, her job is done and she heads back into the water, resuming her life. When the turtles hatch, they make their own way towards the shore, enter the water and paddle out to sea. Their independent life begins.

It's pretty impressive, when you come to think about it. Newly formed and emerging into the world, the baby sea turtle has a nervous system developed enough for it to sense where the water is (they are guided by the moonlight reflecting on the sea), and to co-ordinate their limbs — right off the bat — in order to take them there. They can hunt for themselves, eat what they need, and take shelter in seaweed floats, their 'nursery' for a time.

In contrast, warm-blooded newborns generally require more care. Birds and mammals commonly show intensive parental care of their young, who need time to develop skills for independent living. In relation to body size, birds and mammals have bigger brains than reptiles, and there's a definite link between social connections within a species and brain size: the larger the brain of the species, the greater the degree of parental care required by newborns.

Like humans, chimpanzees form complex social groups, their brains are large in respect to their body size, and newborns rely on caregivers for an extended period. But, in comparison, human infants are especially helpless because their brains are relatively underdeveloped. According to some estimates, the human gestation period would need to be around twenty-one months for a newborn to be at a comparable neurological and cognitive developmental stage to that of a chimpanzee newborn.

The main reason that humans are born in this less-developed state is that the foetus's metabolic demands (calorie intake) can't be met by the mother through placental nutrition after nine months, so we are born extremely vulnerable and dependent: we don't have co-ordinated control of our limbs, we can't propel ourselves from A to B, we can't feed ourselves.

It's a mistake, however, to think of helpless human babies as an evolutionary negative. Being born before the brain is set allows us to learn from experience. We have an extended period of neural plasticity outside the womb, which means we are teachable to a greater degree. Our longer childhood allows us to assimilate complex culture — language, music, dance, social mores, along with fine motor skills for performing dexterous work. Indeed, we are able to wire our brains well into our twenties. Human cognitive abilities have also enabled us to mitigate physical risks through numerous inventions. We are the only species to be able to make fire, for example, which provides warmth, protects us from predators, enables us to cook food, and is useful for host of other things. We've domesticated dogs so we can use them for hunting and protection. And of course, we're very good at developing weaponry.

And here lies a paradox: though humans are adapted for forming complex social bonds and inventing means for promoting their survival, they are exceptional for routinely killing their own species. Humans are, I'm afraid, a particularly murderous group. Other animals, such as chimpanzees, can attack their own kind in revenge as a deterrent to others or to maintain their position in the social hierarchy, but humans take the cake when it comes to killing in revenge. Humans can also spread their revenge far and wide — to include the children or loved ones of an enemy, for example, or to wreak havoc and cruelty on an entirely innocent population not directly related to the original object of revenge. Also, in contrast to humans, revenge occurs shortly after an attack or social transgression — other animals don't spend an extended period of time plotting against enemies.

For all intents and purposes, the human revenge reaction is way over the top, and as we'll see in Part Two, this can also be linked to the extreme dependency we experience in infancy along with our species' unique cognitive abilities.

In the Shadow of Gods—Part II: On Human Frailty and Self-Doubt

The French psychoanalyst Jacques Lacan was particularly concerned with the emotional and psychological implications of our early physical helplessness and dependency. He was also interested in the human capacity for developing and understanding complex language. It is this capacity along with our early dependency that Lacan places at the centre of his psychoanalytic theory. For Lacan, human psychology and psychopathology are intimately related to our unique status as 'speaking beings'.

With social bonds comes language, and while other animals communicate, they don't show anything approaching the sophisticated grammar of human language. Humans might start out uncoordinated and helpless, but we become adept at language very quickly, picking up grammatical rules without instruction. Because of this ability, the linguist Noam Chomsky proposed that a Language Acquisition Device exists in the brain, giving us a natural propensity to learn language. In other words, our capacity to absorb the complexities of human language may be hard-wired in the brain.

Image Makers

The acquisition of language is no small feat: apart from the obvious implications around communication, it also contributes to the human infant developing a self-image; a self-consciousness in the recognition of itself as a subject of language. For Lacan, the infant's sense of 'I' first comes to the fore when he or she can recognise their own reflection. As previously discussed, he called this the 'mirror stage' of development. Humans are one of only a few species that can recognise themselves in a reflection, however Lacan noticed that while the chimpanzee infant (our closest 'cousin') can recognise its reflection earlier than can a human infant, the chimp soon tires of its image, whereas the human is fascinated by theirs. The human infant moves an arm and watches its reflection do the same. It smiles and laughs, and so does the face in the mirror. Amazing!

We recognise ourselves in the mirror and hears our parents' words attached to the image, reasoning, 'That's Sue. That's me'. We've heard the name before, but now we attach it to an image. We now see ourselves as an object — the object in the mirror — and shortly after begin to attribute traits and characteristics to this 'me'. Thus begins a split between the seer and the seen, the subject and the object. Indeed, when a child learns to speak, they often refer to themselves objectively in the third person: 'Sue thirsty. Sue's toy!'

Children build on their image as they acquire language, and they're particularly sensitive to their own name and what is said around it. Everything they hear becomes incorporated into their image. They are the subject of all the narratives around them. For Lacan, this elaborate objectification of the self is the essence of the human world.

We have to wonder at the fascination of the human infant (compared to the chimpanzee, for example) in recognising their reflection. This, said Lacan, was a factor of our greater vulnerability and less-developed state. Inside, the human infant feels a chaotic churning of fragmented thoughts and emotions, but their image suggests they are a whole, stable being. The human infant identifies itself as an ideal, whole, 'I' in the mirror, and thus begins a fascination with the idea of wholeness. They become drawn to images of apparent wholeness because of the fragmentation they feel within.

And thus begins a lifelong process of unconsciously modelling our image on the images of wholeness around us. We make demi-gods of the stronger, more powerful, seemingly more complete people we see, and for infants these gods are their parents, or primary carers — the big, powerful people they rely on for survival. We play parent with our toys as soon as we're able

— the life of adults fascinates us and we yearn to be part of it, to have access to its magic.

Later, we mimic sporting heroes and other invulnerable giants, but no matter who we model ourselves on, we remain acutely aware of our developmental limitations, and we feel insignificant — inferior — because of them. We are small beings in the face of greatness. If a god approves of us, we feel whole; if they don't, we become anxious. We can act out in defiance, or become submissive through defeat. Either way, the powerful figure becomes the centre of our universe, and we orbit around them, forgetting our true self in the process. Our 'I' becomes a precarious thing built on comparisons with the personalities around us, subsumed within their world.

And while we long for approval from our gods, we also wish we had what they had: the power, the glory, the wholeness. We become envious of them, and wish for the recognition they receive by virtue of being 'master'. Perhaps that is the appeal of superheroes: to be able to leap tall buildings in a single bound, to fly unaided through the sky, to block bullets with bare hands. The superhero is our alter-ego, the expression of our longing to be without our vulnerability. Likewise, the appeal of cult leaders and dictators often lies in their seemingly impenetrable self-confidence and absolute narcissism. They appear to be so sure of themselves.

The German philosopher Hegel proposed that the fundamental human need is for recognition, for a self-conscious being to be recognised (deemed important, worthy) by other self-conscious beings. The problem is that we carry our sense of infantile vulnerability well into adulthood. We suffer from the fear of not being good enough, and it's this fear that makes the human species 'exceptional' at killing its own kind.

In my book *Above the Battleground: the Courageous Path to Emotional Autonomy and Inner Peace*, I refer to the work of Dr Joseph Satten, a veteran in the field of forensic psychiatry. In his paper 'Murder without Apparent Motive', Satten examined men convicted of seemingly unmotivated murders and found that the men had become 'triggered' when they felt rejected by the victim. One man, for example, strangled a teenager when he rejected his sexual advances, another beat to death a young boy because he imagined the boy was making fun of him.

The men themselves couldn't understand why they killed these strangers, but all had been concerned about being considered sissy or physically undersized when young, having suffered significant deprivation and cruelty. Their unconscious rage was ignited when the victim-to-be unwittingly triggered the sense of humiliation first experienced at the hands of people more powerful than them.

Extreme examples help shed light on psychological processes within all of us. While our past experiences might differ in intensity, the link between feeling inferior and an impulse to retaliate isn't unique to a childhood characterised by significant trauma. Lacan's point is that we all start out with shame-anxiety, an inferiority complex, by virtue of being human. While other animals might kill to maintain social order, humans have a propensity for killing out of narcissistic fury. The pain of feeling less than others — not worthy of recognition — can lead to a brutal response.

In Hegel's philosophy, our desire for recognition leads us to attack others in an attempt to prove our power and dominance — we use the way of animals to achieve respect and recognition. 'I'll show you!' is the underlying statement. But on another level, our attack is a defence to the painful recognition of our emotional vulnerability and dependency. 'I'm not weak!' is what we're trying to show ourselves.

The pain associated with our self-conscious 'I' might be why some adults continue to talk about themselves in the third person. It often sounds infantile or grandiose when people speak of themselves this way: 'Nobody messes with Bob'. Perhaps for some people, the subjective inner world expressed by 'I' is far too painful to venture into, and talking about themselves in the third person helps to create some distance from it. Third-person speech is particularly noticeable in sportspeople or others in highly competitive fields. The late basketballer LeBron James, for example, announced his decision to join the Miami Heat with the following explanation: 'I wanted to do what was best, you know, for LeBron James, and what LeBron James was gonna do and make him happy'.

Clearly, our early dependency along with the ability to recognise our reflection and our enhanced capacity for language have significant drawbacks. Objectifying ourselves leads to intense self-evaluation, and our heightened self-consciousness becomes linked to feelings of vulnerability, inadequacy and unworthiness. But the situation isn't all bad. This very same self-consciousness can be our ticket to inner peace. In the Buddhist tradition, being born into the animal realm means to be driven by impulse and instinct. In contrast, humans have the ability to consider our perceptions, to question our assumptions and elaborate and reflect upon abstract ideas such as spirit, God and the existential favourite, 'Why am I here?' In other words, with the ability to develop a supremely self-conscious 'I' comes the ability to move beyond 'I, me and mine'.

Awakening from the Dream

According to *A Course in Miracles*, all of our distress comes from guilt. The Course uses the word guilt to encompass both shame and guilt. As such, our distress comes from believing we are bad and inferior, respectively. These exquisitely self-conscious feelings come from a belief that we have attacked God by turning our back on His Oneness, and that we have become a mere shadow of our whole and holy selves.

The first half of life is where we experience a basic retelling of our imagined conflict with God. There's a struggle for autonomy and independence, feelings of weakness and inferiority compared to our parents' omnipotence, wanting to be chosen but forever feeling neglected. It's all there, along with the fear of abandonment and retribution. The first half of life is a Biblical tale.

In the Course's mythology, the belief in our separation from God was the beginning of all self-doubt. We identified with shame, guilt and vulnerability and experienced an acute sense of loss for the love left behind. We felt a void where before we experienced wholeness, and thus began a lifelong search for completion and approval from our various idols. But this search is itself a testament to our neediness — to our weakness and vulnerability — and we became touchy, defensive creatures:

> Only uncertainty can be defensive. And all uncertainty is doubt about yourself.[64]

As Lesson 153 tells us, our safety lies in our attitude of defencelessness, because it affirms the holiness of our spiritual Self. Practicing forgiveness is the way to stop our defensiveness, and it involves three core affirmations: that we are upset because of our interpretations of things; that our mind contains a presence that can provide a different, true, perspective; and, that this perspective will help us see everyone involved — including ourselves — as either coming from love or calling for help.

But because we're very attached to the devil we know — our self-made image — it takes time before we stop looking to the world to placate our vulnerability. We still form special relationships with people and projects in the hope that they will affirm our value, thereby making us feel better. Meanwhile, our true self — both in the sense of our authentic personality and spiritual Self — is lost in the stories associated with our demi-gods, the centre of our childhood universe, later to be projected onto all major relationships.

It takes time and practice to trust that forgiveness really does give us 'everything we want'. Practicing forgiveness is how we avail ourselves of a sense of confidence, stability and peace, enabling us to release our demi-gods from the burden of having to be Everything for us. Yet we often prefer our sense of vulnerability, weakness, shame and guilt, because these things maintain our separate, self-made ego identity. It might be a shabby identity, associated with a great deal of pain, but it's *ours*; we made it. Choosing the weakness of our ego identity over the strength of wholeness reflects our desire to be the author of ourselves, our own authority.

Every idol is a substitute for God, a way of excluding His love. We turn to a special partner, a special project, or a special battle to provide us with reassurance instead. We try to manage our fears by controlling outer circumstances and people rather than asking for help to see things differently, through the eyes of peace rather than judgement. By turning to our idols, we remain in charge. Weak, vulnerable, but in charge.

This is why the Course says that love waits on welcome, not on time. We gradually let go of our idols, along with our investment in feeling weak and dependent, as we learn through practicing forgiveness that we are better off choosing 'the second place to gain the first'. We are much happier without our emotional angst and inner turmoil; happier without a battle to fight, a war to wage, a conflict to feel victimised by or triumphant within, even though that means accepting that we are part of God's Creation, not an autonomous self-made ego.

> It is obvious that any situation that causes you concern is associated with feelings of inadequacy, for otherwise you would believe that you could deal with the situation successfully. It is not by trusting yourself that you will gain confidence. But the strength of God in you is successful in all things.[65]

When we choose to be dependent only on God, which is expressed by practicing forgiveness, we realise our demi-gods are just like us, that they share the same fears and needs. We can then be confident to step into our own shoes — once seemingly usurped by our self-appointed idols — because we're aware that the strength of God, of wholeness, travels with us all.

Between the Sinner and the Saint—Part I: Hegel's Dialectic and Its Relationship to Healing

Robert Mapplethorpe is best known for his powerful black-and-white photographs of flowers in full bloom, and of New York's underground gay BDSM scene. While most people can handle the flowers, many are shocked by the sexually explicit material and close-up studies of male genitalia often hung right beside them. What on earth was Mapplethorpe up to, is a question often posed.

To Mapplethorpe, the flowers and the sexual imagery embodied the same pornographic aesthetic: both subjects were photographed to express an intense eroticism. His cleverness, and perhaps something that adds to the viewer's disorientation, is that he presents his subjects in a way that reflects the symmetry, composition and seriousness of classical art and sculpture. Technically, Mapplethorpe's photos are brilliant. Subject-wise, they remain controversial.

The 'shy pornographer' (as he was once addressed by his long-term partner Sam Wagstaff) is also well known for his portraits of famous people; high-profile artists, writers, actors and musicians all assume a place in his portfolio. Mapplethorpe also created a number of self-portraits that reflected a self-as-dark-entity theme. In these, he is clad in a black leather jacket, his hair slicked up into a quiff, a flip-knife in hand or a cigarette loosely balanced to one side of his mouth: a bad-boy of the Fifties. In one photo he looks like a naked satyr: horns protrude from his head, perhaps in reference to the

Greek god Dionysus (or Bacchus), the god of wine, sensuality, wild abandon and chaos. In another, he stands holding an automatic rifle in front of an inverted five-pointed star, a classic symbol of the devil.

Mapplethorpe liked to identify with the devil because of his (self-described) 'sinful' behaviour. I can imagine him as Caravaggio's Bacchus: a barechested youth with grapes and vine leaves artistically arranged in his hair, holding a glass of wine as he lounges with a gaze that is the antithesis of 'uptight'. German philosopher Friedrich Nietzsche also had a soft spot for Bacchus. So important were Dionysian qualities to Nietzsche's concept of personal evolution and growth, that during his psychological breakdown his identification with the god went into overdrive. Nietzsche wrote a series of letters to friends and royal figures, focussing on the importance of hedonism, sometimes calling for the death of the pope, and signing off as Dionysus.

Both Mapplethorpe and Nietzsche had a strict Christian upbringing. Nietzsche's dad was a pastor, and at elementary school the young Nietzsche was nicknamed 'the little pastor' for his knowledge of the Bible and his piety. Mapplethorpe was one of six children born to a devout Catholic couple, and was brought up in a strict Catholic environment. It's hard not to see the two artists' identification with Dionysus — the sensual, the passionate, the wild — as a reaction against their upbringing. They swung from one pole to another.

The eighteenth-century German philosopher Georg Hegel was particularly interested in this kind of compensation; this swinging from one extreme to another. He saw it in people, but he also saw it in social movements and in the progression of history. To Hegel, the pendulum swing wasn't necessarily a bad thing, but rather a means to a higher end.

Hegel's Dialectic

In his *Lectures on the Philosophy of World History*, Hegel observes that historical progress isn't linear, but is more a series of lurches forward and back between opposite poles. A state of tyranny, for example, generates a need for freedom, but once freedom is achieved anarchy takes over until an element of control is synthesised with freedom, creating a lawful but not oppressive state of affairs.

Hegel described this dynamic — a movement from one opposite to another until a synthesis occurs — dialectical. Specifically, a dialectic is a philosophical term for an argument consisting of a thesis, an antithesis and a synthesis. Both the thesis and antithesis contain parts of the truth, but are gross distortions of the whole. They are exaggerated, unbalanced, and as such are detrimental in particular ways. The pair of opposites interact until they find resolution in a synthesis, whereby the helpful aspects of each become expressed. Here, the whole is certainly greater than, and different to, the sum of the parts.

And so, the world makes progress by lurching from one extreme to another, as each movement seeks to compensate for a previous mistake. The Enlightenment (1715–1789), for example, was a period in European history which grew out of the seventeenth century's scientific revolution, and which elevated the value of human reason. The world could be understood through a rational process, and this meant an end to a focus on mystery, intuition, the authority of the Church and an emphasis on supernatural beliefs.

The Romantic era followed as a reaction against the Enlightenment, stressing the importance of feeling and the irrational in human life. A sense of respect for what can't be measured or contained came back onto the scene, though it led to a degree of wildness and excess in the name of free expression. As these two camps wrestled with each other (a kind of 'science versus the arts' situation), a middle stance emerged that recognised our need to appreciate both reason and emotion, deduction *and* poetry.

Likewise, we can all achieve a greater sense of inner unity through a dialectic: you could say we reach a greater appreciation for our wholeness via the exploration of opposing aspects, first divided out and clearly seen, then integrated in a way that expresses their helpful aspects.

For Hegel, such a synthesis (within ourselves or in the greater social field of history) wasn't just about working things out on the worldly plain. Hegel was also a student of theology, and created a metaphysical explanation for what he observed, giving his dialectic a much grander function than simply achieving a 'happy medium'.

Hegel's Metaphysics of Polarity

In *The Phenomenology of Spirit*, Hegel describes the historical dialectic as the bi-product of an all-encompassing mind or spirit that is coming to understand itself. 'In the beginning', according to Hegel, there was an abstract unity consisting of spirit, or mind. Although this was a unity, it was in its infancy, not knowing itself as well as it could, not quite all it could be. To reach a higher unity, spirit underwent a series of divisions into separate functions, and thus was born a universe of opposites: spirit and matter, light and dark, freedom and restraint, inner and outer; the list goes on.

The most important dialectic in Hegel's metaphysics is that between master and slave. The master is a particular consciousness that's in conflict with its antithetical consciousness, the slave. The master wants to dominate, the slave wants to be free, and so there is an ongoing struggle between the two. A synthesis occurs when both the master and slave realise their interdependence, and this happens when they realise their inherent equality. After all, the master is also a slave of sorts because they depend on the slave's labour.

Basically, when master and slave see their common humanity, this is a step forward in matter being reunited with spirit, and toward spirit understanding itself. This realisation also brings with it a true sense of freedom — of independence through interdependence. If we are all united in spirit, or mind, then my dependence on you is my dependence on me. As Hegel put it, the synthesis in the master-slave dialectic involves a realisation of 'The I That Is We, and the We That Is I'.

Hegel's philosophy is known as idealism, because he believed that the master-slave dynamic would work itself out through time until there would no longer be any masters or slaves, and eventually no world or universe, just spirit as a higher form of abstract unity.

In Hegel's metaphysics, the creation of a world of opposites out of a primordial unity happens so that the Absolute can realise itself better. The metaphysics of *A Course in Miracles* also contains a creation myth based on splits and division. However, the Course differs significantly as to cause and purpose, and this leads to a different idea of what synthesis means and how it can come about.

A Tiny, Mad Idea

In the Course's creation myth the world is the result of a mistaken belief that we could separate ourselves from Oneness. The myth begins with an abstract unity: God as Love, Knowledge, Oneness. At some point it appeared as if a part of God's Oneness pondered on the possibility of being a separate entity, and what it might be like to have a will of its own. And with this thought, the imagined situation seemed to become a reality; this part of God's Oneness now perceived itself as separate from the All, and opposed to it.

This separated aspect then had two thoughts, or heard two voices: one that said that it had indeed separated from God, and one that said nothing had happened, because it *couldn't* happen. The former was the voice of what the Course calls the ego, the latter the voice of the Holy Spirit, our memory of unity. According to the Course, all of us who believe we are here (that's *all* of us!) listened to the ego, but then felt guilty for having destroyed God's Oneness, becoming fearful of punishment.

Having believed the ego, we forgot all about the Holy Spirit voice. We therefore didn't turn to the Holy Spirit for help with our fear, but instead tried to get rid of it by projecting the imagined conflict with God out onto a world governed by opposites of all kinds, eternally at war with each other. And regardless of how things look to observers in terms of who is a victim and who is a victimiser, who is a master and who is a slave, all of us will identify as the victim at some level: 'Look what you made me do!' is the cry of many people observed abusing others. The drive to identify as the victim is the drive to keep our guilt at bay.

In the metaphysics of the Course, division is the result of repression. The 'tiny, mad idea' that we could separate ourselves from Oneness leads to guilt and fear of punishment. We then repress our guilt and project out a world of opposites in which to hide, identifying as a victim impinged upon by people and circumstance of the world around us. And we find victimisers everywhere, in every way, shape, and form; the ego's voice teaches us that our peace is held to ransom by things outside of our mind, outside our agency. This is what makes us feel victim to the stock market, the boss, our partner, parents, children or the food we just ate.

Victims and victimisers: this thesis and antithesis are the Course's equivalent of Hegel's master and slave dynamic. The hammer and the anvil, the winner and the loser, the self-effacing compliant type and the domineering defiant type — there are so many ways you could put it — but it's the one dynamic that relentlessly makes the world go round.

If we look at any extreme — the defiant sinner, or the self-effacing saint — there's a repression behind it related to our separation from God, which means there's a call for healing. Synthesis then, in the Course's system, is a matter of forgiveness, and this will be explored in Part Two of this post.

Between the Sinner and the Saint—Part II: Hegel's Dialectic and Its Relationship to Healing

The Course's metaphysics are in line with psychological theory: behind a dissociation — or split into opposites — is repression of an issue, an inner conflict related to incidental or developmental trauma. It's like a train travelling along a track until it reaches a point (a trauma) where the track suddenly splits in two. The train itself then splits in two so that half goes down one track — the conscious, expressed aspect of the personality — and half goes down the other track, representing its unconscious polar opposite.

We adopt the conscious track in order to feel safe. For example, if we were belittled, made to feel inferior, ignored, or mocked for our sensitivity, we might adopt a tough guy suit of armour, leaving our feminine side to coast down the unconscious track. Conversely, if we're treated in a way that leads us to fear authority figures and being 'bad', or if we suffer a trauma that makes us afraid of our spontaneity and self-expression, we can develop a compliant, submissive attitude. In turn, anything resembling self-care and assertiveness heads down the unconscious track.

Repression, Splitting and the Original Trauma

In the Course's myth there are two reasons we experienced God as an 'unloving father'. Firstly, we wanted Him to give us special attention, but He couldn't because specialness of any kind goes against the very constitution of Oneness. Secondly, we resented the fact that God created us: *we* wanted to have the power of First Cause. We wanted to be Number One in terms of attention and power. We wanted to feel adored above all else, to be king of the mountain.

These issues with God are translated into our earthly experience through our first relationships with authority figures — our parents or primary carers. Wanting to be adored above all else translates into sibling rivalry; resenting the power of your parents relates to the authority problem. The first scenario involves a fear of abandonment and rejection (shame-anxiety), the second a fear of punishment (guilt-anxiety).

Sigmund Freud is known for his emphasis on repression — how it develops in regard to our relationships with parents, and how it plays out in our lives, particularly in psychosomatic complaints. Carl Jung is better known for an emphasis on splitting and dissociation — on the two tracks that develop out of the repression. Perhaps the clearest indication of how these two approaches relate to healing is seen in their views around dream interpretation. Freud looks at dreams as a way of fulfilling a wish that we can't fulfil in our daily life, and this wish will also express something Oedipal in nature — we want to possess the affections of someone we shouldn't, and/or take a rival down a peg or two. We want to seduce, or we want to destroy: that's about the sum and substance of our wishes according to Freud.

Jung takes another approach to interpreting dreams. He sees them as compensation rather than a means for wish fulfilment. To Jung, our dreams compensate for our conscious attitude by showing us the qualities we have dissociated and that are calling for integration. The qualities we have repressed are given a voice in our dreams.

Freud and Jung also differ on why dreams tend to be so bizarre. Freud explains the weirdness of dreams (they don't obey the laws of space and time, they can be full of contradictions, they can jump from a beginning straight to an end) as a mental censor that guards our sleep: by expressing our unacceptable wishes in a disguised form, the dream protects the sleeping ego.

In contrast, Jung, sees the symbology of dreams as a way of expressing the compensatory attitude that is trying to emerge, and the weirdness of dream imagery as the result of their emergence from a level of the mind where meaning is created through metaphor and symbol. There is, says Jung, no attempt to disguise anything in a dream.

Jung gives the example of a female patient's dream in which someone gave her a richly ornamented antique Celtic sword. In analysis, she associated the sword with a dagger that belonged to her father. In writing about this dream (*On the Doctrine of Complexes*, CW. Vol. 2) Jung suggests Freud would say the dagger represented the patient's wish for her father's 'weapon'. In other words, the interpretation would have a sexual slant, representing the daughter's wish to possess her father sexually. Jung puts forward his own view: the sword represents the patient's need to express the wholeness of her personality. It is a compensation for her own passive and dependent attitude via a symbolic image of passion, energy and will.

We could, however, also see the sword as related to the patient's father, in that it represents his Celtic ancestry and powerful position in the family. The important point is that the object is a sword, not a dagger, and though related to the father, represents something stately and warrior-like. This is in contrast to a dagger, with its more underhanded, sinister, possibly murderous connotations. The sword, therefore, could indicate the patient was ready and willing to embody the healthy, majestic aspects of will and self-assertion, which is not the same as a desire for dominance and control over others. It is distinct from a 'kill or be killed' mentality, which perhaps had been evident in her father.

The difference Freud and Jung's theories on the function of dreams is also reflected in their views of artistic creativity, which is highly symbolic by nature. Art, according to Freud, is a way for the artist to sublimate their sexual drives, and seek (unconsciously) for fame, money and 'the love of a woman'. Jung has a very different view of artistic creativity: art can be seen as a way of representing something that is in the process of becoming known.

The work of David Bowie provides a clear example of the Jungian view of creativity. Early in his career, Bowie wrote and performed music under the guise of several alter egos. Ziggy Stardust was Bowie's first major stage character and made his debut with the 1972 album *The Rise and Fall of Ziggy Stardust and the Spiders from Mars*. Ziggy was an androgynous alien rockstar sent to Earth to save the world from the apocalypse. In true rockstar form, however, he ends up being more interested in seduction, taking up the mantle of lover rather than fighter. After touring the album in the US, Bowie was ready for a change in character. Aladdin Sane (a-lad-insane) was born as the alter ego of Ziggy; a dark and sinister character, followed by the equally dark Thin White Duke, who became known for his extreme right-wing sympathies.

After his time as the Thin White Duke, Bowie started to embrace his uncurated self as a performer, and the stage personas went by the wayside. In interviews, he describes being unprepared to perform on stage as himself until he'd explored these various characters. Moreover, his exploration wasn't limited to writing music and creating costumes. For instance, when Bowie was working on a song, he'd often use painting as a way to move forward when he felt blocked or unsure of how to proceed (*Charlie Rose*, March 31, 1998). His combined artistic endeavours were clearly a way of giving form to something he was processing within himself. A painting, they say, is always a self-portrait, and Jung would agree. This is perhaps why many artists would still do what they do even if there wasn't any financial reward. They do it because they have to; it's their means of integration, of achieving a synthesis between the thesis and antithesis playing out internally.

This is why I suspect we gain so much pleasure from some works of art: there is something in them that we recognise within ourselves, our own process of coming to terms with our contradictions, along with the promise of the ever-present whole. In a video *How to Listen to Music* (PS Music Berlin, 2014), Daniel Barenboim, the great contemporary conductor and pianist, said that people find solace in sad music (hello, Schubert) not because it makes them sadder, but because great music contains all emotions. It can be sad yet contain happiness at the same time; it expresses one aspect whilst connecting with the whole.

Synthesis

If Robert Mapplethorpe's fascination with the satanic, the sinful and the darkly erotic was at all a reaction to his upbringing, I wonder how his art might have evolved if he'd had long enough — beyond his forty-two years — to work through his conflicts with his father Harry. As illustrated in reporter Kim Master's interview with Harry one year after Robert's death (*Harry Mapplethorpe, a Father's Tale,* Washington Post, 1990), Harry was never able to accept his son's sexuality or bohemian lifestyle, and he was resentful that Robert didn't provide for him at all in his will, donating much of his wealth to the Getty Museum and programmes for artists and AIDS research.

In so many ways, Robert fell far from the tree. Harry Mapplethorpe was a staunch conservative who had never, and would never, vote Democrat. In his retirement he ushered at mass every Sunday and maintained his membership with the National Rifle Association, storing his collection of rifles in Robert's old bedroom.

An engineer, Harry had wanted his sons to follow suit, and was discouraging of Robert's interest in art as a career. Get a nine-to-five job, get married, have children: that was Harry's way. After Robert moved out of home in his late teens and headed for New York to pursue a career as an artist, he returned to the quiet, middle-of-the-road suburb of his parents, wearing black leather and accompanied by punk rocker and poet Patti Smith, his similarly bohemian partner. Harry wasn't impressed:

> The way she used to dress and the way he used to dress — I used to think, 'How have they got the nerve to come here like that?' This is a quiet neighbourhood. I used to get so aggravated... I probably passed some remarks about his dress and things of that sort...

Not only did Harry not approve of Robert's lifestyle, he thought his pursuits were 'unmanly'. When asked by Masters whether he would consider going to a Patti Smith concert, Harry replied scornfully, 'That's not for men'. The rock scene, the art scene, the bohemian life — none of it was the 'natural' preoccupation for real men. At least, that was Harry's stance.

The disdain for Robert's lifestyle and career choice, along with rejection of his sexuality, might have created a cocktail of shame for Robert, who exhibited a level of self-destructiveness in his cavalier attitude toward the risks of contracting HIV. For many people whose identity is significantly linked with shame, a 'bring it on' attitude toward physical danger and their own demise is common.

Robert remained absent from his family for years after his initial return, keeping a distance and focussing on his work. Even when his brother Richard died, he didn't attend the funeral. It wasn't until 1987, when Robert's parents found out he was dying of AIDS that they first visited his studio loft in Manhattan. Harry was impressed by his son's collection of fine art and the opulent surrounds, yet quietly resented that the life his son had led contributed to his illness. But the subject of Robert's lifestyle was never broached; they talked about his art collection instead.

Robert had kept away from his family because he knew his father, and perhaps his mother, wouldn't be able to accept his sexuality and his work, yet I wonder how much this effort to keep separate fuelled his obsession with dark places. Was it, in some way, an attempt through defiance to feel strong — the leather-clad self-portraits a form of subterfuge for a sensitive, vulnerable, hurt individual. Was the sexually explicit material an attack on the sensibilities of a father more concerned with the opinions of his 'quiet neighbourhood' than making his son feel welcome?

In Hegel's dialectic, the swinging between opposite poles of historical movements occurs over centuries until some kind of synthesis is reached. In other words, it takes a very long time to attain a happy medium; things lurch one way then the other until we understand how to make them work for the better. On an individual level — in matters related to our own psychological experience — it might take decades, a generation, or lifetimes before we work things out this way. There simply aren't enough hours in the day, or years in a lifetime, to get the job done. If only there was another way.

Forgiveness: Saving Thousands of Years

Returning to the psychological idea — also expressed in the Course's myth — that repression precedes splitting and the adoption of an extreme position, it follows that working through the repression will help us come to a more balanced position, a synthesis of the harmonious aspects of the poles. Conversely, you could say that alongside every major forgiveness issue stands the adoption of an extreme.

The process of addressing a significant grievance is often initiated through some kind of calamity or challenge to our habitual way of doing things. This is the stuff of myths and movies. For example, a career-obsessed parent who has no time for their child nearly loses them in an accident. Then, after days by their child's bedside in hospital they come to see how important they are to them. The child recovers, the achievement-oriented parent is born anew, more balanced and caring. It sounds cliché but it resonates with us time and time again because on some level we know this kind of transformation touches on something essential to our own being: an extreme character (in one respect or another) experiences a calamity which necessitates self-reflection and growth, and a more balanced character is born.

In my book *Above the Battleground: the Courageous Path to Emotional Autonomy and Inner Peace*, I describe how Patty Schemel, the drummer for punk rock band Hole, went through such a transformation after a humiliating experience in the recording studio, in which her musicianship, her value, was questioned. She had been sober for months, but after leaving the studio — feeling humiliated, betrayed, confused and professionally uncertain — she reached for comfort in drugs. She left the band and rented a room where no one (including her family) could find her.

Subsequently, Schemel's drug and alcohol use went to a level it hadn't gone to before. She became addicted to heroin and crack. She became homeless, turning to theft, prostitution and selling drugs to feed her habit. Not only was the addiction a means of numbing her emotional pain, Schemel's self-destructive behaviour was a (self-confessed) 'Screw you, guys!' towards everyone who had let her down. In her demise she pointed an accusing finger at all who had abandoned and mistreated her in her near present and distant past. There was, moreover, a strong element of self-pity in her self-destructiveness, along with a tacit agreement of the lowly opinion she believed others had of her.

Growing up in the Seventies, Schemel had been teased for her red hair and glasses, and she knew that her sexuality strayed from the norm. She got the message from the wider culture that she should be ashamed of herself and began to feel lonely and stupid in public. The incident in the studio brought all of Schemel's childhood humiliations home. And they hit her with an almighty thud. Indeed, her autobiography is titled *Hit So Hard*.

When she finally decided she'd had enough of street life, Schemel phoned her father then stayed with him while she joined a rehabilitation programme which addressed her past, her self-concept and her addictions. And while drumming had once been Schemel's way of channelling her aggression and feeling powerful, it became a means of assisting her recovery — she became a drumming teacher for children and teens.

Schemel's experience expresses something of the nature of synthesis. When we're no longer stuck in an extreme (either self-destruction or self-elevation) we express what is both helpful to ourselves *and* to others: we experience something akin to Hegel's 'The I That Is We and the We That Is I'. What we do then has a sense of community about it, even if we're working on our own, or in seeming opposition to something (as part of a political group, for example). We do what we do, but we embody a caring nature that is neither self-effacing or domineering. We are truly helpful.

Importantly, Schemel's recovery also involved a spiritual aspect related to the Twelve Step recovery programmes she attended. At the end of the day, the repression behind all repressions is the one involving our relationship to God. Our poor self-concept stems from a belief that He rejected us, that He regards us unworthy. As we practice forgiveness towards those we hold responsible for our lop-sidedness, or defensive character armour, the blocks of shame and guilt that keep us fearful of God are removed and we come to remember our true relationship with Him. And as we accept our sameness with each other — that we are all suffering from a belief in our unworthiness, yet also share the same holy Self — we are released from the ego's tyranny of comparisons.

This is why the Course's process of forgiveness can save us thousands of years, so to speak. Instead of going backward and forward between extremes until we recognise our wholeness, inherent connectedness and equality (a realisation that is the foundation of Hegel's synthesis), we can experience this in any given moment through connecting with our Inner Teacher and practicing forgiveness:

> The miracle substitutes for learning that might have taken thousands of years. It does so by the underlying recognition of perfect equality of giver and receiver on which the miracle rests.[66]

Because our ego identification is the ultimate source of our distress, we don't need to bring every grievance (or every case of conflicting opposites within us) to light in order to let them *all* go:

> It is not necessary to follow fear through all the circuitous routes by which it burrows underground and hides in darkness, to emerge in forms quite different from what it is.[67]

We don't have to look at absolutely everything that has been repressed, however, there will be one or two special people with whom we need to address our shame and guilt:

> Should one brother dawn upon your sight as wholly worthy of forgiveness, then your concept of yourself is wholly changed. Your 'evil' thoughts have been forgiven with his.[68]

After working with specific issues in our lives, we will begin to accept the more general idea that our lack of peace comes from clinging to our special, separate ego identity, having turned our back on God's all-inclusive Love and the inherent equality of Oneness:

> Yet it is necessary to examine each one as long as you would retain the principle that governs all of them. When you are willing to regard them, not as separate, but as different manifestations of the same idea, and one you do not want, they go together.[69]

The Holy Instant is the moment in which we choose forgiveness instead of shame and guilt, and identify with the wholeness of our Self. We can imagine what it would be like for the Holy Instant to be our only instant, using a musical metaphor. In music, more than one voice (note) can be heard and appreciated at the same time: this is called harmony. Recently, I listened to Under Your Spell – Standing (Reprise) from the musical episode of Buffy the Vampire Slayer. The song starts with actor Amber Benson singing a sad, touching melody. Anthony Head then joins in the singing and together the harmony creates a beautiful, vibrant depth. I can imagine this to be only a hint of what it's like when the Holy Instant is our only instant: as we sing in harmony with ourselves, each other, and God's Will, we experience the vitality of wholeness.

Notes

THE INNER PILGRIMAGE

1   T-31.V.17:2, 6-7

2   T-31.V.17:8-9

3   T-31.V.17:3-5

4   T-13.III.1: 4-6, 11

5   T-13.III.2:1-3

6   T-18.VII.7: 7-9; 8:1-3

THE THORN IN YOUR SIDE

7   M-26.3:1-2

8   M-26.3:1-2

PAIN AND THE BRAIN

9   T-26.V.5:4

RELEASE THE HOUNDS

10   T-19.IV.A.11:2; 12:6-7

11   T-19.IV.A.5:3-4

12   T-19.IV.A.14:4

13   T-26.VIII.4:3-4

14   T-26.I.2:5

15   T-13.VIII.4:3-4

THE PRESENT MEMORY

16   T-18.VI.11: 1, 3-7

17   T-1.II.6:2-4; 8

18   T-22.V.3:11-12

19   T-18.IV.1:9

THE COOKIE MONSTER

20 W-123.2.1:2-4; 2:1
21 T-13.X.1:2, 4
22 T-17.III.1:2-3

THE JONAH COMPLEX AND THE NEED TO BELONG

23 T-17.VI.2:1-3
24 T-17.VI.4:1-3;5
25 T-6.VB.1:1-2

DREAM WORLDS

26 T-18.I.4:4
27 T-27.VII.11:6-8
28 T-27.VII
29 C-3.4.1
30 T-26.V.5:4
31 W-155.1:1-3

THROUGH THE LOOKING GLASS: FORGIVENESS, TIME AND THE EVENT HORIZON

32 T-26.III.2:1-6
33 T-22.II.6:1; 6-7
34 T-22.IV.1:1-6
35 T-1.I.13:1-3
36 T-13.VIII.5:4
37 W-107.2:1-5;3:1

THE SCRIPT IS WRITTEN: SYNCHRONICITY AND THE MIND-WORLD CONNECTION

38 W-158.4:3,5
39 T-13.I.3:5-7
40 W-pII.13.1:1-3
41 T-14.IX.3:2-3

KLEIN AND A COURSE IN MIRACLES: ON LOVE, LOSS AND THE CENTRALITY OF THE ATONEMENT PRINCIPLE

42 T-13.in.2:5-6;8-9
43 T-21.I.5:1-2
44 T-5.IV.1:2;4;7-8
45 T-25.II.6:8

46   T-5.IV.8:2-6;15

SEEING THE PROBLEM AS IT IS—PART I: KAREN HORNEY'S DEFENSIVE SOLUTIONS
47   T-23.II.2:1-3

SEEING THE PROBLEM AS IT IS—PART II: KAREN HORNEY'S DEFENSIVE SOLUTIONS
48   T-6.V.B.1:1-2
49   T-31.II.3:3-5;4:1-3
50   W-153.2: 3-6
51   W-153.4:1
52   W-153.6:1-3
53   W-39.4:1-2

PLAY SCHOOL: THE WORLD AS TRANSITIONAL OBJECT
54   W-29.2:3-4
55   W-29.3:1-6

THE ONLY TRUE REFLECTION
56   W-93.1:1-2
57   W-159.3:4-5
58   T-4.IV.2:2-3
59   T-14.IX.5:4-6
60   T-14.IX.5:1
61   T-14.IX.7:1;4
62   T-14.IX.6.5-8
63   W-159.3:1-3

IN THE SHADOW OF GODS—PART II: ON HUMAN FRAILTY AND SELF-DOUBT
64   T-22.V.3:11-12
65   W-47.5:2-4

BETWEEN THE SINNER AND THE SAINT—PART II: HEGEL'S DIALECTIC AND ITS RELATIONSHIP TO HEALING
66   T-1.II.6: 7-8
67   T-15.X.5:1
68   T-31.VII.2:5-6
69   T-15.X.5:2-3

About the Author

Stephanie Panayi has worked as a counsellor and Rolfer™, graduating from the Rolf Institute® (USA and Brazil) in 1998, and from Swinburne University (Australia) with a degree in psychology and psychophysiology, in 2004.

Stephanie came across *A Course in Miracles* in 1997, and integrated the Course's principles within her professional practice. She now enjoys writing from a Course perspective about a range of topics related to the business of being human.

Also by Stephanie Panayi

Reflections on 'A Course in Miracles': Volumes One to Three

Combined Volumes One to Three of *Reflections on 'A Course in Miracles'*: A deep dive into the Course, covering work, relationships, creativity, and all the barriers to being your true self.

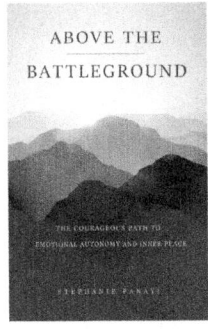

Above the Battleground: The Courageous Path to Emotional Autonomy and Inner Peace

'I wish I hadn't got so upset!' These words are familiar to all of us. Why do we go on automatic pilot when we feel rejected or unfairly treated, retaliating with an outburst that we later regret? And why are there similarities in the course of our relationships with friends, partners, and jobs?

Above the Battleground explores the origins of our most intense emotional needs and how they send us into self-defeating battles to have them met. Using psychological theory, principles from *A Course in Miracles*, and examples from the author's clinical experience, *Above the Battleground* provides a unique take on the origins of our deepest insecurities along with a way to rise above them to achieve a sense of security, happiness and peace.

Made in the USA
Middletown, DE
21 July 2021